Traditional Witches' Formulary and Potion-making Guide

Recipes for Magical Oils, Powders and Other Potions

Sophia diGregorio

2012
Winter Tempest Books

Copyright © 2012 Sophia diGregorio

All rights reserved.

ISBN-10: 0615727484
ISBN-13: 978-0615727486
Winter Tempest Books

DEDICATION

In memory of my grandparents.

	Part I: How to Make Powerful Potions	
1	About the Formulary	3
	Magic the Esoteric Science	5
2	How to Increase the Strength of Your Potions	7
	Incantations and Languages of Power	8
	Timing According to Planetary Correspondences	20
	The Planetary Hours	22
	Timing by Phases of the Moon	24
	The Moon in Astrological Houses	25
	Sabbats	26
3	Augmenting or Altering the Formulas	27
	Making Substitutions	30
	List of General Substitutions	33
	Herbs and Their Properties	35
	A-C	35
	D-F	41
	G-L	43
	M-Q	46
	R-Z	50
	Herbs Classified by Planet	55
	Herbs Classified by Zodiac Signs	62
	Quick Color Guide	65

Part II: The Potions

4	Inks of Art	69
5	Conversion of Oil, Incense, Powder and Wash Formulas	75
6	Oils	79
	Elemental Oils	128
	Sabbat Oils	130
	Planetary Oils	133
	Zodiac Oils	137
7	Old Traditional Potions	141
8	Powders	161
9	Incense	197
10	Washes and Baths	211
	References	217
	Abbreviations and Conversions of Measurements	221

Part I
How to Make
Powerful Potions

Sophia diGregorio

1 ABOUT THE FORMULARY

The Traditional Witches' Formulary and Potion-making Guide is a reference to help you create powerful magical potions. It contains more than 300 individual formulas for oils, powders, ink, incense and washes from different magical practices and traditions along with information about beneficial timing, incantations and other aspects of potion-making. Most of the formulas given here employ natural ingredients with the exception of a few old traditional formulas and those that call for food dyes as colorants.

Some of the formulas are derived from very old ones, which contained ingredients that are presently unknown, unavailable or highly toxic. In such cases, reasonable substitutions have been made in accordance with the formula's purpose.

The author has attempted to choose ingredients for these formulas that are not too difficult for the modern western practitioner to find. Of course, availability will vary depending on your own geographical location. But, if ingredients are not available locally, they are usually available through on-line stores.

A few herbs, some of which are mainstays in classic formulas, are unavailable for purchase in certain jurisdictions. If a particular herb is not sold in your area, you may have to either make a substitution or gather the herb instead of purchasing it. You will see a reference here for how to choose a good substitute when an ingredient is unavailable to you.

Wherever possible, practitioners should try to grow and gather their own herbs and other ingredients. It is a widely accepted belief that the process of growing, harvesting in accordance with astrological timing and processing herbs with directed intention increases their potency.

Warnings: Please, bear in mind that just because an ingredient is natural or not widely recognized as toxic, this doesn't mean it is safe for all people. Any herb can cause an adverse reaction in some people.

For instance, there are people who are allergic to the entire mint family. Although, plants from the mint family are not generally thought of as being toxic.

Some herbs and especially their essential oils are not safe for human consumption. A few of the ingredients in these formulas are caustic and should be handled with care. None of the formulas in this book are intended to be consumed with the exception of the legendary love philter Love Potion No. 9.

Where such an ingredient is given, the author has tried to place a warning about it. But, there is no way to guarantee a potentially dangerous ingredient has an adequate warning. If you are in doubt about an herb or ingredient, check its safety before consuming it or applying it to your skin.

Many essential oils and some herbs (including those with names ending in "bane") cannot be safely consumed. Essential oils should never be applied to infants, toddlers under approximately three years of age or to cats. Pregnant and nursing women should, also, take special precautions and completely avoid some herbs and oils as they can affect the delicate hormone balance resulting in grave danger or death.

Magic the Esoteric Science

All world religions, including those which profess opposition to magic or witchcraft, include some form of magical practice that includes communication with or manipulation of unseen forces. Such practices may involve communicating with spirits or gods, healing, harming or otherwise affecting the environment by supernatural means.

Apart from differences such as language or pantheons, the practice of magic around the world is strikingly similar, although, often it is not a religious practice, but a natural one. Magic is so similar world-wide because it has a basis in esoteric science.

Esoteric science differs on many points with contemporary, orthodox science, although both consist of operational theories, by which we try to explain the nature of the world. Esoteric science is no less valid than orthodox science, which is in many ways still as dogmatic and hostile towards "heretics" as it has been in centuries past.

Historically, institutions of government and religion condemned, ridiculed and outright forbade the use of this occult knowledge for the common masses, while hypocritically practicing it themselves in secret. It has been both protected and disseminated at different times through secret orders and now, in the Age of Aquarius, it is open to anyone who has the desire, perseverance and strength of mind to seek it out.

Esoteric science is one consisting of vibrational harmonics and frequency ranges. It posits that a dynamic energy (the fifth element or the ether) runs throughout the cosmos on different planes, permeating all things. It is the medium through which subtle electronic pulsations pass, which carry information and make all things possible, both seen and unseen.

Typically, there are two important physical elements in a potion: Minerals and herbs. Some minerals are naturally present in herbs. Some potions include metals or gemstones to enhance their mineral content. They act like a battery within the potion, imparting the elements of fire and water, which are the basis for life energy. Herbs direct the flow of this energy, as do other items added to potions along with incantation and intention.

All people, animals and things emanate an individual vibrational harmonic, including minerals, herbs, the planets and even the words we use. Ingredients combined in a potion at a particular time, in conjunction with focused intent and words of power all combine to create a potent substance, which can then be used to effect change in the physical world.

To create successful potions, it is important to keep in mind this idea of harmonic frequency emanations of all things in the universe.

2 HOW TO INCREASE THE STRENGTH OF YOUR POTIONS

Before you begin making a potion, it is a good idea to cleanse your work space and yourself both physically and spiritually. Ideally, the place where you choose to do your work along with the instruments and vessels you use in the entire process should be cleansed and sanctified to your purpose.

Before beginning, you might find it helpful to take a bath with a few drops of essential oils such as Rosemary, Lavender, Hyssop, Bay, Basil or Rose or Lemon. Doing so will refresh you and clear any low level vibrations that might interfere with the business at hand.

This is optional, however, it is beneficial to work while you are in a calm state of mind. Potions are made more efficacious and their energies are better directed by you when you are able to keep your mental focus on what you're doing.

You may cleanse any unwanted energies from your home or work area using a simple smudge, using a White Sage bundle. You might follow this up with the burning of a Sweet Grass braid to invite helpful spirits back in. Sweep the room with a broom with the intention of sweeping out the dirt and dirty, disharmonious energy.

Anoint your altar, work space or home with a blessing oil and say a prayer to clear adversarial energies and request the assistance of spirits who can help you.

Reciting incantations or words of power and inscribing powerful symbols on your tools and vessels may help to keep you in the proper state of mind and encourage energies harmonious with your purpose.

Incantations and Languages of Power

Incantations are used to cleanse your work space, direct energy and imbue your potions with increased power. There is power in both the written and spoken word. Some languages are more powerful for magical workings than others. Those most commonly employed in spells and rituals are Latin, Old Norse, Old Saxon, German and Hebrew.

Both Hebrew and Old Norse are ancient languages conceived to facilitate communication with the gods.

The Norse Runes and the Theban Runes (Witches' Alphabet or the Runes of Honorius) are commonly inscribed on tools, vessels, candles and other objects of ritual to direct and increase their power.

The Psalms of the Old Testament which are partially attributed to the ancient Hebrew sorcerer King Solomon and his father David the Giant Slayer, also, contain power words hidden within them. Each Psalm has a specific purpose, which can be found in *The Books of Moses*. These psalms, which are incantations as much as they are prayers, appear to retain their power even in English and are sprinkled with power words or "names of God" all throughout.

The words and languages you choose are up to you, but, you should be able to feel their power when you use them. Ultimately, the most important aspects of any incantation are that it helps keep your mind focused on your work and it speaks to to the intelligence of the things involved in the process to affect and direct their energies to your purpose.

Along with these power words are invocations and evocations to the powers of gods, angels, demons, saints, ancestral spirits and elementals to guide you and empower your work. The choice of these is a personal one and each practitioner should choose whichever entities best suit him or her.

To begin, choose the space you want to work in. Most often practitioners create potions in their kitchens. Cleanse or exorcise the space using power words and stating your intention.

For example:

"By the Power of the Most High, I command all adversarial spirits out!"

Sanctify and dedicate your instruments. Say a blessing over the knives, vessels and herbs you plan to use. You may even inscribe a blessing upon them. Such powerful words spoken over the tools, vessels and ingredients during the process of creating your potions gives them greater strength and help to clearly define their purpose. Some potion-makers set aside and consecrate certain items in their kitchen just for the purpose of making potions.

Objects used in the manufacture of your potions may be fumigated using a purifying incense like copal or sandalwood. Pass the object through the smoke while reciting your incantation. For example:

"By the eternal power of the Five Elements, be purified and strong. Be dedicated to steadfastness, that through you, my will shall be done." (Wiccans may want to add to this statement: "...and no harm shall come to anyone.")

Speak to the herbs. State your intentions with powerful words. Tell them what you want them to do as you combine them and are grinding, stirring or brewing.

Each individual herb can be spoken to and addressed as follows:

"[Name of herb] be thou sanctified and dedicated to the purpose of [state your purpose]."

The *Grimorium Verum* provides incantations for the sanctification and blessing of the instruments involved in the manufacture and use of a pen and ink of art, which illustrate how incantation is used to cleanse and consecrate every item used in a potion. It, also, shows an example of how the vessels and instruments involved in the making of potions should be chosen and prepared according to the principle of astrological timing.[1]

According to the old ceremonial magicians, every article to be used in a magical operation should be consecrated. The following examples are for consecrating the pen, ink holder and the ink, which will be used in potion or spell. Note the use of power words or "names of God" in capital letters.

A new quill or pen should be fumigated by passing it through incense. When you prepare a quill for writing, hold it in your hand and recite the following incantation:

"ABABALOY, SAMOY, ESCAVOR, ADONAY. I have expelled all illusion from this pen, that it may retain efficaciously within it the virtue necessary for all things which are used in this Art, as well for operations as for characters and conjurations. Amen."

The bottle and ink well should be prepared in the Planetary Hour of Mercury and in that very same hour, the words, "JOD, HE, VAU, HE, METATRON, JOD, CADOS, ELOYM, SABAOTH," should be written upon it. Only then should it be filled with ink which has been exorcised.

Exorcism of the Ink

The *Grimoirum Verum* gives an elaborate incantation, complete with Kabbalistic power words for the exorcism of the ink, as follows:

"I exorcise thee, creature of ink, by ANSTON, CERRETON, STIMULATOR, ADONAY, and by the name of Him Whose one Word created all and can achieve all, that so thou shall assist me in my work, that my work may be accomplished by my will, and fulfilled with the permission of God, Who ruleth in all things and through all things, everywhere and for ever. Amen."

This is a very powerful incantation that can be adapted for all of your tools or even potion ingredients by substituting such words as "creature of the elements," "creature of earth," "creature of steel," or whatever the case may be for "creature of ink" as a form of address to the object you are charging. This incantation invokes the protection and assistance of powerful ancient beings in clearing the item of adversarial energies and focusing it to your purpose.

Benediction of the Pen

In the following prayer, wherever you see the "+" symbol make a cross in the air over the ink using your index and middle fingers while holding your thumb against your pinkie and ring finger. This benediction may be adapted for use in blessing other potions and tools.

"Lord God Almighty, Who rulest all and reignest through all eternity, Who dost fulfill great wonders in Thy creatures, grant unto us the grace of Thy Holy Spirit by means of this pen. Bless it +, sanctify it + and confer upon it a peculiar virtue, so that whatsoever is said, whatsoever we desire to do and to write herewith, may succeed through Thee, Most Holy Prince ADONAY. Amen."

After pronouncing this incantation over the object, asperge it by sprinkling it with Holy Water, fumigate and exorcise it.

When a pen or quill for writing is first obtained, consecrate it to its magical purpose by saying:

"ABRACHAY, ARATON, SAMATOY, SCAVER, ADONAY! Expel all evil from this feather, so that it may possess full power to write whatsoever I will."

If it is a quill, shape it with a knife of art, which has likewise been consecrated to that purpose. Pass the quill through incense and asperge it on the Day and during the Hour of Venus. Then, inscribe the following words, using an inscription tool, which has previously been consecrated, as well:

"JOD, HE, VAU, HE, MITATRON, JAE, JAE, JAE, CADOS, ELOYN, ZEVAO."

When you dip the pen into the ink, exorcise and consecrate it by reciting this incantation:

"I exorcise thee, creature of the feather kind, by ETERETON, by STIMULATON and by the name ADONAY. Do thou aid me in all my works."

Once the items to be used are prepared, you may prepare yourself for the work at hand by reciting this incantation:

"Lord God, ADONAY, who hast formed man in Thine image, I, the unworthy and sinful, beseech Thee to sanctify this water, to benefit my body and soul, cause me to be cleansed."

The preceding examples, which are all from the *Grimoirum Verum*, illustrate how the energy in each and every object involved in an operation may be bent toward your purpose by means of power words and incantations. These examples may be used by traditional witches and ceremonial magicians as they are or changed to better suit your needs and personal taste. For example, Wiccans may prefer to alter it by substituting the names of their own deities, elements or words of power for the names of god printed in capital letters. It is your choice how far you will go with this, but you can see that historically magicians have used incantation to empower every single component involved in a magical working.

To create your own incantation for any potion, write down your purpose on a piece of paper and create a short phrase to say as you prepare it. You may use an old incantation, a mantra, your own words or some combination of these things.

Keep in mind that the word "incantation" means to sing and enchant. So, whatever you choose should help you to generate power and focus your intentions on the creation of your potion.

The following are examples of incantations you may use as they are, alter or augment as it suits your purpose:

Abracadabra

It is believed that the incantation, "Abradabra," comes from the Aramaic for "Create as I say." It's first known appearance in literature is found in the Liber Medicinalis, which dates back to the 2nd century A.D. In *The Book of the Law*, Aleister Crowley states that the proper spelling is "Abrahadabra."[2]

It is a power mantra that can be said at any time to increase the power of a potion or spell. The word may be used alone or added to any other incantation.

Exorcism Incantation

The following is an ancient Christian oration in Latin, which is very powerful in expelling evil influences. It inscribed upon the medal of St. Benedict. Despite the

Catholic Church's centuries old war on witchcraft, many practices within the church, such as their Rites of Exorcism bear a strong resemblance to magical practices.

"Crux sacra sit mihi lux,
Nunquam draco sit mihi dux,
Crux Sancti Patris Benedicti,
Vade retro Satana! Nunquam suade mihi vana!
Sunt mala quae libas. Ipse venena bibas!"

General Incantation for Potions

"Spirits hear me! And obey!.
At this time, in this hour,
Manifest your hidden power.
By the power of the elements, so be it!"

Healing Potions and Unguents Incantation

Repeat Psalm 6:2: while making healing preparations:

"Have mercy upon me, O Lord; for I am weak: O Lord, heal me; for my bones are vexed."

The above Psalm and many others are used by Hoodoo and Santeria practitioners as well as some old folk healers of northwestern European descent. In the Ozark mountain region passages of the Bible are read in hospital rooms where ailing patients lie to speed their healing. Although numerous passages from the books of the Bible are used as prayers and incantations in various spells, the most commonly used are the Psalms.

In the Kabbalistic grimoires, the *Sixth and Seventh Books of Moses*, various uses of the Psalms are given, which may be incorporated into the making of potions for those specific purposes. For example, some Psalms are intended to provide protection from enemies or success in business.

Love Potion Incantation

"Bind these souls in love
A love that is sublime
Send power from above,
Bind them for all time."

Use this incantation as it is or combine it with the names of powerful love goddesses as is done in the traditional incantation for Love Potion No. 9.

Money Potion Incantation No. 1

The following is a Sanskrit mantra dedicated to Lord Kubera, the Hindu god of money. It contains powerful sounds. Repetitiously, sing each syllable evenly on one note.

"Om Shreem Om Hreem Shreem Hreem Kleem Shreem Kleem Vitteswaraay Namah."

The first nine words are pronounced exactly as you see them, however, the last two are pronounced like "Vit-es-wah-ray-yah Na-mah-hah." Like the Obstacle Breaking Incantation given below, this mantra can be sung while you are preparing your potion or before. It is very powerful when sung on single, low note and has a similar effect to the rhythmic beating of a gentle drum on the psyche.

Money Potion Incantation No. 2

"Destroy all worries, destroy all sorrow.
Destroy all need to beg and borrow.
Let abundance and wealth flow free,
By the Power of Earth and Sea,
As I say, so mote it be!"

Your incantations do not necessarily have to rhyme. You can, also, chant using single or multiple names of power from specific runes that suit your purpose.

The most important part of any magical operation is not its origins, but its efficacy. Approach potion-making as an experiment. Always note what brings you the best results so you can perfect your craft. Once you have an incantation you like for any of your potions, write it in your magical journal or Book of Shadows alongside the formula and other details, so you will remember it.

Obstacle Breaking Incantation

This is a mantra to the Hindu god Lord Ganesha. It is valuable for clearing the obstacles to success. Recite it over herbs and potions you are creating for this purpose.

"Om Gam Ganapataye Namah"

It is pronounced like, "Aum Gam Gah-nah-pah-tah-yea Na-ma-hah."

This mantra is really powerful any time and you may find it useful for getting your in the proper mental state before making potions. The syllables are sung, similar to how a Catholic priest sings at mass, except they are sung on a single note. Chose a note low or high where your voice is comfortable to you and sing it, dragging the sounds out so that it is pronounced in one exhale. It is customary to repeat a mantra 108 times, which may take 10 minutes, if sung properly.

Peace and Harmony Potion Incantation

This is a simple incantation or blessing that can be used by any witch, although it may have special appeal to Wiccans. Hermeticists will recognize the god and goddess as the representation of electromagnetic polarity, which is needed to charge the potion with your intention.

"God/Goddess bless this brew
With vibrations of harmony, peace and love.
By the universal power, so be it."

As you pronounce these words over your potion, imagine the forces of fire and water combining to make an electromagnetic force, impregnated with your will. See this going into the potion as you mix it.

Quitting Potions Incantation

The following is called the Merseburg Incantation after the name of the cathedral library in which it was found. It dates back to the High German period of the 8th or 9th centuries, but it is likely far older. Use this incantation over herbs and potions intended to release a person from the bondage of another person or institution. This includes Quitting potions, hex and spell-breaking as well as Get Out of Jail potions.

"Eiris sazun idisi,
Sazun hera duoder.
Suma hapt heptidun,
Suma heri lezidun,
Suma clubodun,
Umbi cuoniouuidi.
Insprinc haptbandun,
Inuar uigandun."

Victory and Success Incantation

The following incantation, called the "Carmen Arvale," is well-known to many Wiccans. The word "Carmen" comes from the old Roman word for verse and is, also, used to denote a prayer or charm. Like Hindu mantras, they are to be sung nine times over herbs and prayers used in potions for success, domination and other endeavors involving the planet Mars and its fiery influences.

"Enos Lases iuvate,
Enos Lases iuvate,
Enos Lases iuvate."

"Neve lue rue Marmar sins incurrere in pleoris,
Neve lue rue Marmar sins incurrere in pleoris,
Neve lue rue Marmar sins incurrere in pleoris."

"Satur fu, fere Mars, limen sali, sta berber,
Satur fu, fere Mars, limen sali, sta berber,
Satur fu, fere Mars, limen sali, sta berber."

"Semunis alterni advocapit conctos,
Semunis alterni advocapit conctos,
Semunis alterni advocapit conctos."
"Enos Marmor iuvato,

Enos Marmor iuvato,
Enos Marmor iuvato."

"Triumpe! Triumpe! Triumpe! Triumpe! Triumpe!"

A Final Word on Incantations

Whether you choose ancient prayers, chants or mantras or whether you choose to make your own words, rhyming or not, the most important aspect of an incantation is that it imbues the potion with power and purpose. While there are traditional incantations that have reached a stage of importance in folk lore, such as the incantation of the nine goddesses for Love Potion No. 9, there really are no hard and fast rules when it comes to reciting words over potions.

It is important that an incantation give power to a formula in a way that is not a hindrance to you. If you focus on the words to such an extent that you forget to keep your attention on what you are doing this could be problematic. Or, if you are so distracted by chanting that you fail to project a strong level of psychic energy into the potion's manufacture, then you should definitely forgo the idea.

Certainly, if you find yourself very mentally focused without aide of an incantation, there is no need to keep chanting words as you work. Those who are practiced at meditation and mental discipline and who know how to gather their mental energies and focus them will likely find this ability more valuable to supercharging a potion than any incantation.

While this is really another area of discipline, it certainly applies here and mentioning it may prove of value to the novice. One way to categorize the potion one is brewing is to consider it along the lines of the four elements: Fire, water, air and earth. The potion can then be mentally charged accordingly.

Potions of a fiery nature may be imbued with passionate, electrically charged energy by the maker. Potions of a watery, emotional or drawing type may be charged with this magnetic energy. Those of an airy nature, pertaining to growth, abundance and success may be charged with the powers of air. Those of a more material nature may be charged with earth. Most potions benefit from being charged by a combination of these, which is impregnated by the maker with his or her intention.

As another form of incantation, some practitioners like to speak a few simple words of encouragement to the herbs in some way, either mentally or verbally as they add them to the potion. Yet another way to make an incantation without distraction is to wait until the moment that you combine the ingredients are mixing them together to say a few words of empowerment over the potion.

While the vibrational harmonics inherent in the potion ingredients is extremely important, the maker's intention plays a valuable role in strengthening and directing those energies and even supplying them with subtle nuances.

Timing

To maximize the potency of your potions, choose an auspicious time for the gathering of your ingredients. Many modern gardeners and farmers are aware of the importance of timing for planting and harvesting of plants. They know that planting seeds according to the planetary phases makes the difference between an average harvest and abundant one. Likewise, for more efficacious potions, make them according to the timing of the planets and the phases of the moon.

Two excellent publications for determining the right times to plant, harvest and prepare potions are as follows: *The Old Farmer's Almanac*, Yankee Publishing, Dover, New Hampshire(www.almanac.com); and *The Witches' Almanac*, The Witches' Almanac, Ltd., Newport, Rhode Island (witchesalmanac.com).

The Old Farmer's Almanac is available at ordinary department stores in the U.S. Unfortunately, *The Witches' Almanac* is not as widely available or as well known. It is unique among almanacs because it begins the New Year on Beltane.

Timing According to Planetary Correspondences

The planetary hours are an ancient, Western system of organizing human affairs using the traditional seven planets. Each planet has a corresponding day to which each kind of potion and its purpose can be classified.

For example, love potions should be made in the hour of Venus; Court Case potions in the hour of the Sun or Mars; wealth potions should be made during the hour of Jupiter, potions for binding and cursing should be made during the hour of Saturn, etc.

Choose the best day to make your potion based on its purpose as follows:

Sun (Sunday): Potions for success; fame; illumination; learning; vitality; family; dealing with authority figures, success in business matters and influencing court cases.

Moon (Monday): Potions for the mind; mental health; the home; meditation; prophetic dreams, divination, increased intuition, planting and harvesting and affecting time.

Mars (Tuesday): Potions for increased passion; vigor; aggression; courage; adventure; the triumph of the will; success in military actions; law suits; conflicts; sports and conquering.

Mercury (Wednesday): Potions for communications; higher learning; occult studies; business; acting; the arts; sales and marketing; writing; short trips; deception and con artistry.

Jupiter (Thursday): Potions for prosperity; abundance; growth; expansion; increase; optimism; increased earning; good luck; healing; psychic development and expansion of awareness; investments; settling disputes and giving blessings.

Venus (Friday): Potions for love; friendship; other affairs of the heart; charity; social situations; parties; gatherings; weddings; engagements; romance; beauty and communications with women.

Saturn (Saturday): Potions for binding; shrinking; restricting; decreasing; marriages; contracts; legal matters; to break a habit; chronic illnesses; older people; the dark arts; cursing; hexing, hex breaking; revenge and spell reversal.

The Planetary Hours

After you have chosen the most beneficial planet for the type of potion you plan to create, then find the proper planetary hour.

The fastest way to calculate planetary hours is with a Planetary Hours Calculator. These little software programs are available at web sites online and as Smartphone applications. You can find your planetary hours for the day or night in an instant. But, you can do it manually, as well.

The day is divided by the daylight hours and the nighttime hours. Each planetary day begins at sunrise and ends at sunset. Each planetary night begins at sunset and ends at sunrise the following day.

Each part of the planetary day is divided into twelve equal "hours." The same is done for the night. You will have 24 unequal hours between day and night. Rarely will any of your hours actually consist of 60 minutes.

As you can see from The Table of Planetary Hours, which is given below, the first planetary hour of each day corresponds to the day, itself. For example, the first planetary hour of Sunday is always the hour of the Sun; the first planetary hour of Monday is always the hour of the Moon, and so on.

The hours repeat infinitely in the following order: Sun; Venus; Mercury; Moon; Saturn; Jupiter; Mars.

Determine the time of sunrise and sunset for your particular geographic location.

Calculate the number of minutes between sunrise and sunset and divide the sum by 12.

Choose the correct day of the week on the Table of Planetary Hours.

Determine each planetary hour for any minute of the day according to the 12 planets listed under that day.

To calculate the planetary hours for night time, do the same procedure only instead calculate using the number of minutes from sunset to sunrise.

Table of Planetary Hours

Hour	Sun.	Mon.	Tues.	Wed.	Thurs.	Fri.	Sat.
1	Sun	Moon	Mars	Mercury	Jupiter	Venus	Saturn
2	Venus	Saturn	Sun	Moon	Mars	Mercury	Jupiter
3	Mercury	Jupiter	Venus	Saturn	Sun	Moon	Mars
4	Moon	Mars	Mercury	Jupiter	Venus	Saturn	Sun
5	Saturn	Sun	Moon	Mars	Mercury	Jupiter	Venus
6	Jupiter	Venus	Saturn	Sun	Moon	Mars	Mercury
7	Mars	Mercury	Jupiter	Venus	Saturn	Sun	Moon
8	Sun	Moon	Mars	Mercury	Jupiter	Venus	Saturn
9	Venus	Saturn	Sun	Moon	Mars	Mercury	Jupiter
10	Mercury	Jupiter	Venus	Saturn	Sun	Moon	Mars
11	Moon	Mars	Mercury	Jupiter	Venus	Saturn	Sun
12	Saturn	Sun	Moon	Mars	Mercury	Jupiter	Venus

Timing by Phases of the Moon

The moon has a powerful effect on the earth's energies. Many practitioners believe the moon phase is one of the most important considerations in the timing of magical endeavors. Consult an almanacs or use Moon Phase software or applications to determine the current phase.

Determine the best moon phase during which to create your potions based on their purpose.

New Moon: This phase runs from the first day of the new moon to 3 1/2 days after. It is a good time to brew potions for new beginnings and new ventures including new love affairs, new businesses and the formation of new habits.

Waxing Moon: This phase begins 7 days after the new moon and lasts for 7 days after. It is the right time to brew potions for positive purposes such as increased money and prosperity, to gain something you want, to acquire love, to foster friendships, to improve health, wealth, luck, love and success.

Full Moon: This phase begins 14 days after the new moon and lasts 3/12 days. It is a good time to make potions for divination, protection, love, legal matters, financial betterment, increased energy and empowerment.

Waning Moon: This phase begins 3 1/2 days after the full moon and lasts for 10 1/2 days. It is the right time to make potions for the dark arts, to bind, get revenge, break a habit and to banish a problem, a pest, enemy or an unwanted lover.

Dark of the Moon: This phase begins 10 1/2 days after the full moon and lasts for 3 1/2 days. It is the right time to make a potion for getting rid of bad habits and for banishing, binding, justice and revenge.

The Moon in Astrological Houses

Another way to determine the best time to create a potion is based on the characteristics of the moon in the following astrological signs.

The aforementioned almanacs give the signs of the moon throughout the calendar year and some web sites offer "Moon Sign Calculators" you can use to determine the position of the moon for any day of the year.

Moon in Aries: Potions for money; to get a job; increase sales; improve business; for strength; courage and passion. Avoid the creation of potions for divination at this time.

Moon in Taurus: Potions for matters pertaining to love; financial matters; real estate and practical, every day matters.

Moon in Gemini: Potions related to travel; communication; sales; acting; public relations and healing.

Moon in Cancer: Potions related to the home; loyalty; intuition; sympathy; fertility; family and children.

Moon in Leo: Potions for fame; careers; success; to gain power over others; for courage and childbirth. Avoid the creation of potions for love or relationships at this time.

Moon in Virgo: Potions revolving around learning; healing; employment; health; the intellect; security and stability.

Moon in Libra: Potions pertaining to legal matters; marriages; court cases; partnerships and peace keeping.

Moon in Scorpio: Potions for divination; necromancy; psychic experiences; psychic development; spirit communication; the dark arts; secrets; power and sexual matters.

Moon in Sagittarius: Potions involving travel; publishing; athletic events and learning. Avoid making potions for divination or psychic enhancement at this time.

Moon in Capricorn: Potions for domination; career; politics; ambition; material wealth; control and stability.

Moon in Aquarius: Potions for healing; peace; harmony; freedom; science; to find creative solutions and for understanding.

Moon in Pisces: Potions for divination; astral travel; spirit communication and emotions.

Sabbats

The eight Sabbats are times when powerful cosmic rays strike the earth. You may choose times on or near these dates to create your potions for added potency.

Beltane or May Day: April 30th

Litha, Midsummer's Eve or Summer Equinox: June 21st

Lughnassadh: August 2nd

Mabon or Autumn Equinox: September 21st

Halloween or Samhain: October 31st

Yule or Winter Equinox: December 21st

Imbolc or Candlemas: February 2nd

Ostara or Spring Equinox: March 21st

3 AUGMENTING OR ALTERING THE FORMULAS

Traditional formulas contain certain ingredients that make them what they are. Examples of such basic formulas are Van Van, Hot Foot, Goofer Dust, Love Potion No. 9, Four Thieves and Florida Water. Certain ingredients cannot be left out of these formulas or they cease to be authentic.

Many of these formulas are very old. You may see more than one formula for a particular purpose in this book. This is because different practitioners like to add their own touches or modify a formula for a particular purpose.

A common way to augment formulas is to make them more potent or to increase the speed of their actions.

You can do this to any of the formulas by adding a portion of the following herbs, as they suit your purposes, to the potion:

Ingredients To Strengthen or Speed the Action of a Potion

Almond Oil
Black Pepper
Balm of Gilead

Blood (especially menstrual blood)
Caper
Cascara Sagrada
Chile Pepper
Cinnamon
Cloves
Coconut Oil
Graveyard Dirt
Lemon Verbena
Myrrh
Sea Salt
Senna
Van Van
Vanilla
Witches Burr

Because of its potency, Almond oil is frequently recommended as a base oil throughout this book. In the case of most formulas (except Van Van), you may substitute a different, light, natural base oil. Because of its stability, Jojoba is commonly used as a base in cases where potions are going to be stored for a very long time.

Other Items Used in Potions

Along with herbs and minerals, other items that represent the purpose of a potion may be incorporated at the potion maker's discretion. For example, potions for curse reversal or dark arts may include the hairs of a black dog or cat. Black cat hairs are, also, sometimes used in spells for invisibility or to change luck.

Objects that represent an idea in some way may, also, be included. For example, a broken necklace chain may be added to potions intended to end a relationship. Unraveled hemp cord may be added to crossing and hexing formulas.

Nail clippings, hair, urine, semen, blood and particularly menstrual blood is sometimes used in potions designed to dominate another person or a situation. It is used both in love potions and in those designed to make another person do something, such as move away or leave you alone.

Graveyard dirt is commonly used for protection, domination and dark arts potions. Some practitioners ascribe a great deal of importance to how it is collected, especially for particular purposes. Typically, it must be obtained at midnight. Often, the gatherer of the dirt digs down, at least, six inches and leaves a small coin as payment in return for taking a small portion of the soil. Graveyard dirt used for malicious purposes is best gathered at midnight from the graveyard of a murderer or suicide victim. Graveyard dirt is used in both protective and hexing formulas.

Dirt from a crossroad is sometimes used to add the element of confusion to a potion. Ant hill dirt, collected carefully from the nest of stinging ants, is used in potions and spells to make an unwanted person depart.

Red brick dust is used is some Hoodoo spells to impart protection. It is obtained from old-fashioned red brick that is crushed and pulverized. Sometimes the bricks are smudged with sage to purify any negative energetic attachments from the past.

Baked and powdered white eggshells (Cascarilla Powder) are used for purification and protection. They are, also, used to mark the body and the ground, as well as for other purposes in spells and rituals.

Sea Salt is a common ingredient in potions and serves to enhance the power of a potion, although, it carries its own powers of purification and consecration. It is used to clear crystals, ritual tools and to purify the energy around hour altar, work space and both inside and outside your home. It is blessed and consecrated and used to enhance purifying baths and washes, It may be used to gain control over another person or situation and is used in spells to obtain employment, curse, banish and, also, to heal.

Soot and ashes are ingredients in banishing and other potions for darker purposes. The chemical element sulfur, archaically called "brimstone," is, also, commonly used in formulas for banishment, domination or dark arts.

Black Salt (Witch's Salt) is a variation on sea salt,

wherein it is combined with charcoal, ashes or other blackening substance. It is a sprinkling powder used to drive away unwanted spirits or people from a place, to dominate and hex.

Naturally magnetic stones and magnetic sand are used in potions intended to draw money or love.

The bark of trees that have been struck by lightning is used in spells to destroy enemies. Powdered seashells and crushed insects are used to hex and curse.

You may use any other items that you feel accurately represents the purpose of your potion. Save "gifts" given to you by insects and animals in the form of hives, shells, spider's webs, feathers, remnants of claws or whiskers, which are naturally created and then shed or abandoned by these creatures. Incorporate such things into potions according to their nature.

Making Substitutions

There is a lot to be said for studying old, tried and true potion formulas, however, it is often the case that ingredients that were common 100 years ago are difficult or impossible to find today. Some are toxic or come from animal sources, which are unnecessarily cruel. When making a substitution, the most important thing to keep in mind is the purpose of the ingredient.

Your changes should be informed and based on the ingredient's natural properties and purpose. To replace an herb in a formula, choose a substitute with similar metaphysical properties, if possible, from the same astrological or planetary category as the original one. A list of some herbs followed by their astrological properties is given below.

If you cannot find the herb in the list below, suggested substitutions are categorized after it by planet and zodiac sign. This is not a comprehensive list, nor is it applicable to every potion. Therefore, it should only be used a general guideline. If you are adept with the pendulum and you must choose between two or more options, dowse to determine the most appropriate ingredient.

A Few Common Substitutions

Cassia and Cinnamon are essentially the same thing, although Cassia refers to the leaves of the tree and Cinnamon usually refers to the bark. These can usually be substituted for one another in a formula, although, this is not always a good substitution. Always consider the purpose of the ingredient you want to find a substitute for.

Mullein is sometimes substituted for Graveyard Dirt. Copal and Frankincense are commonly substituted for other resins. Rosemary is sometimes substituted for Frankincense. Rose is sometimes used as substitutes for other flowers.

Tobacco leaves are sometimes substituted for Sulfur, Aconite (Monk's Hood or Wolf's Bane) Datura, Belladonna and other plants of the Nightshade family as well as other poisonous herbs such as Hemlock.

Citron, Lemon Balm, Lemongrass, Lemon Verbena, Lemon and Orange may often be substituted for one another in potions. Orange, Orange flowers and Tangerine can be substituted for one another.

Mints can often be substituted for one another in a potion, especially Peppermint, Spearmint and Wintergreen. Basil, Lavender, Oregano, Rosemary, Thyme and Catnip are, also, from the Mint family and may be substituted for one another in some potions.

Peppers may sometimes be substituted for one another.

Some old formulas call for musk, but most musk oils available today are synthetic and do not contain the proper energetic properties. One form of true musk used in some old formulas is Beaver Castoreum Tincture or Castoreum Perfume. It is used by some perfumers and may be available from perfume supply houses. Castoreum is made from the dried, preserved gland of the male beaver. It is used in love and attraction potions and is an important ingredient in some classic Hoodoo formulas.

Similar musks used in old formulas are True Musk

derived from the glands of the Musk Deer and Civet, which is derived from the glands of an African cat. These have become difficult to obtain. Ambergris and Ambrette (Musk) Seed are commonly substituted. Synthetics are not recommended because they do not contain the proper energetic properties and may be toxic to human health and the environment. The species of deer and cats used in the production of these musks are endangered.

Love, lust and seduction potions in this book use Ambergris as a substitute for animal musks. Ambrette seed may, also, be used. In very old formulas, the original ingredients are given, but the possible substitutions are noted for your convenience.

Creosote is coal tar, it is used in some old Hoodoo formulas. But, it has become difficult to obtain in both the U.S. and the U.K. Although, it is still available to farmers and gardeners. It is the sticky substance produced when coal is burned. It is used in potions to make things stick to the subject of the spell. Some botanicas and Hoodoo supply houses sell tar balls, which are made of the sticky tar in street pavement. When this cannot be found, other tar oils or very sticky substance may be used. Other items used is spells for binding and hexing include turpentine and lodestones. Herbs like Devil's Shoestring , Couchgrass, Byrony and Ivy can be used to bind the spell to the subject.

Ammonia is a purifying and cleansing ingredient, which is sometimes used to replace urine in a potion.

In general, plants which are part of the same species or have similar physical properties may be good substitutes for one another. The following list of substitutions should be approached only as a guideline. Your own informed discretion and understanding of your potion's purpose should be the strongest considerations when making substitutions.

List of General Substitutions

Acacia Gum: Gum Arabic
Amber: Sandalwood
Asafoetida: Valerian and Tobacco
Balm of Gilead: Rose or Gum Mastic
Benzoin: Gum Arabic or Gum Mastic
Calamus: Vetivert
Camphor: Eucalyptus or Lavender
Carnation: Rose and Cinnamon
Cedar: Sandalwood
Clove: Mace or Nutmeg
Clover: Five Finger Grass
Copal: Frankincense or Cedar
Cypress: Juniper or Pine Needles
Deer's Tongue: Tonka Bean; Woodruff or Vanilla
Dittany of Crete: Gum Mastic
Dragon's Blood: Frankincense and Sandalwood combined
European Mandrake: Ginseng
Eucalyptus: Camphor or Lavender
Five Finger Grass: Clover or Trefoil
Frankincense: Copal or Pine
Galangal: Ginger or Cinnamon and Mace combined
Grains of Paradise: Black Pepper
Gum Arabic: Frankincense or Gum Mastic
Gum Mastic: Gum Arabic or Frankincense
Hellebore: Tobacco or Nettle
Hemp: Anise; Bay; Damiana or Nutmeg
Hyssop: Lavender
Ivy: Five Finger Grass
Juniper: Pine
Mace: Nutmeg
Mint: Sage
Mistletoe: Mint or Sage
Mugwort: Wormwood
Musk (Castoreum, True Musk, Civet, etc.): Amber (Ambergris) or Ambrette (Musk) Seed
Neroli: Orange
Nutmeg: Mace or Cinnamon

Oak Moss: Patchouli
Patchouli: Oak Moss
Pepperwort: Black Pepper; Grains of Paradise or Rue
Pine: Juniper
Rose: Rosehips
Sandalwood: Amber
Sarsaparilla: Sassafras
Sassafras: Sarsaparilla
Sulfur: Asoefetida; Club Moss or Tobacco
Tobacco: Bay
Tonka Bean: Deer's Tongue; Vanilla Bean or Woodruff
Trefoil: Five Finger Grass
Valerian: Asafetida
Vanilla: Deer's Tongue; Tonka Bean or Woodruff
Vetivert: Calamus
Woodruff: Deer's Tongue or Vanilla
Wormwood: Mugwort
Yew: Tobacco

While many ingredients and formulas are tried and true and known for their reliability, most practitioners customize their formulas through informed and inspired experimentation.

Use an experimental approach when making formulas. Let your intuition be your guide. If you want to use a little more of an ingredient in your formula try it and see if you like the results. If you feel the formula could benefit from including other ingredients, this is a good way to add subtle nuances or give direction to a formula.

If a formula calls for a powdered herb or resin, but you only have the essential oil, you can usually substitute an oil for the dry ingredient form of the herb in a formula.

If a formula calls for an essential oil, but you only have a dried or powdered form of the herb, you can usually use this as a substitute. Dried, powdered herbs are usually allowed to infuse in oil for, at least, a couple of weeks before they are strained.

The main objective is to get the energetic influence of the ingredient into the potion. Below is a list of herbs and their properties.

Herbs and Their Properties

A-C

Abre Camino (Eupatorium villosum or Koanophyllon villosum): Road opener
Acacia (twigs and bark): Money; new love; psychic powers; protection and physical strength.
Acai Berry: Powerful dreams and increased psychic powers
Adam & Eve Root (Arum maculatum): Love; happiness and binding
Adder's Tongue: Healing; especially bruises and wounds
African Ginger: Mental focus
African Violet: Release harmonious love vibrations.
Agaric: Fertility.
Agave (Thorn): Effigy magic; used for magical inscriptions
Agrimony: To reverse a curse; courage and for protection from serpent bites
Alfalfa: Good luck and to prevent poverty
Alkanet: Money; prosperity and purification; success in business and gambling
Allspice (Pimento): Good luck; prosperity; courage and success in business
Almond: Money and prosperity
Aloe Vera: To expel evil; protection of home and business
Aloes (Bitter Aloes): Love; spirituality; to banish; to expel evil
Althea: Protection and increased psychic powers
Alum: Stop gossip and slander.
Alyssum: Protection and temperance
Amaranth: Protection; invisibility and to heal from heartbreak
Amber (Ambergris): Courage; longevity; success; lust; inspiration; psychic powers and wealth

Ambrette (Musk Seed or Hibiscus Moschatus): Aphrodisiac; calming and relaxing
American Sweetgum (Liquidambar Styraciflua): Protection
Anemone: Protection and healing
Angelica: Love; prophesy; reverse bad luck; banish rivals; exorcism; impart creativity and inspiration
Anise: Youthfulness; divination; psychic ability; protection from the evil eye; luck and gambling
Apple: Love; healing; happiness and immortality.
Apricot: Love.
Arbutus: Exorcism and protection from evil
Arrow Root: Gambling and good luck.
Asafoetida (Asafetida or Stinking Gum): Protection; purification and exorcism
Ash Bark: Prosperity and protection.
Ash Tree: Prosperity; protection and good health
Aspen: Eloquence; to prevent theft; to keep a lover from being stolen.
Aster: Love
Avens: Love; purification and exorcism
Avocado: Love; lust and beauty
Bachelor's Buttons (Cornflower): Psychic development and love; worn to attract romance
Balm: (See Lemon Balm)
Balm of Gilead: Manifestations; protection from evil; and increases the strength of a potion
Bamboo: Money; prosperity; good luck; protection for the home or business
Banyan: Good luck; fertility and good health
Barley: Love and fertility
Basil: Love and to keep a lover faithful; protection and exorcism; wealth and success in business
Bat's Head Root: Protection from black magic and the evil eye
Bay Leaves: Job success; promotion; pay raise; money; insight; purification and prayer
Bayberry: Money and wealth; finding a job
Bedstraw: Love

Beech: Love and tolerance
Beet: Love and good health
Bell Heather: Inner resolve and confidence
Belladonna (European): Flying ointments; visions and astral projection (Poison: Do not ingest.)
Benzoin (Benjamin): Steady flow of money; steady employment and astral projection
Bergamot: To command and control; aphrodisiac
Be Still (Thevetia nereifolia): Protection (Poison. Do not ingest.)
Bilberry (Huckleberry): Protection; luck; hexing; hex breaking; spell reversal and powerful dreams
Birch: Protection; purification and exorcism
Bing Cherries: Divination and love
Birth Root (Beth Root or Dixie John): Luck; love; marriage; romance; sex and ease of childbirth
Bishop's Weed: Protection from snakebite and to provoke lust
Bistort (Snakeweed): Money; wealth; fertility and to increase psychic powers
Bittersweet: Protection and to heal a broken heart
Blackberry: Money; protection; visions and healing
Black Beans: Protection
Black Eyed Peas: Money and good luck in the new year
Black Helebore: Protection from evil (Poison. Do not ingest.)
Black Pepper: Confidence; hexing; to cause quarreling and promote ill-feelings
Black Root (Culvers Root): Purification
Black Seed or Kalonji (Nigella Sativa): Banishing; hex breaking; curse reversal and exorcism
Black Snakeroot: Love; lust and wealth
Bladderwrack (Seawrack): Money; protection; travel; visions; dark arts; hexing and to call winds
Bleeding Heart: Love and divination regarding love
Blessed Thistle: Home protection and protection from evil
Bloodroot: Love; purification; protection and to reverse spells
Bluebell: Prosperity and good luck; to get to the truth

Blueberry: Protection and vivid dreams
Blue Cohosh: To attract love
Blue Bonnet: Gambling and good luck
Blue Flag: Money
Bodhi: Protection; fertility; meditation and mysticism
Boneset (Ague Weed): Protection; exorcism and to curse an enemy
Borage: Strength; courage and increased psychic powers
Bracken: Divination and prophesy
Brazil Nut: Love
Briony: Money; protection and effigy magic
Broom (Broom Top): Clarity; concentration and improved intuition
Broomcorn: Exorcism
Bromeliad (Crypanthus): Money; protection; divination; purification and to call the wind
Buchu: Prophesy; powerful dreams and increased psychic powers
Buckthorn: Protection; exorcism; court cases; contracts; legal matters and to make wishes come true
Buckeyes: Good luck; prosperity; gambling; luck in love
Buckwheat: Protection
Byrony: Binding
Cabbage: Good luck
Cactus: Protection and to get a job
Calamus (Sweet Flag): To dominate a person or situation
Calendula (Pot Marigold): To win in court; luck in the lottery and prophetic dreams
Camellia: Love and luxurious wealth
Camphor: Divination; spiritual cleansing; healing and past lives
Caper: Lust and luck; to increase potency of potions
Caraway: Lust; protection from thieves and increased psychic powers
Cardamom: Love and lust
Carnation: Love; strength and protection from evil
Carrot: Lust; fertility and health
Cascara Sagrada: Court cases and to speed the action of a potion

Cashew: Money and prosperity
Cassia Leaf (Cinnamon): Luck and money
Castor: Protection and healing
Cat Tail: Lust
Catnip: Love; beauty; happiness; relaxation; to make an unfaithful lover faithful again
Cat's Claw (Una de Gato): Youthfulness; healing and protection
Cayenne: Exorcism
Cedar: Purification; money and protection
Celandine: Court cases; to repel black magic; cause confusion; protection from law enforcement agents and to evade prosecution
Celery: Lust; increased mental powers and psychic abilities
Centaury: To repel snakes and break fevers
Cerato: Self-confidence
Chamomile: Purification; harmony; good luck; money; wealth and restful sleep
Chaste Tree Berries (Vitex): Love and fertility control
Cherry: To enhance psychic powers; clairvoyance and dreams; creativity; love and healing
Chervil: Spiritualism and communication with the dead
Chestnuts: Love and a peaceful home
Chickweed: Love and fertility
Chicory: To receive favors; increased psychic abilities; invisibility and road opening
Chili Pepper: Love; hex breaking; fidelity and to expedite the action of a spell
China Berry: Good luck and to make changes
Chives: Protection and weight control
Chrysanthemum: Protection
Cinchona: Protection and good luck
Cinnamon (bark): Power; confidence; lust; fast money; aphrodisiac and speeds the action of potions
Citron (Xiang Yuan): Psychic powers
Citronella (Citronella Pelargonium or Cymbopogon Nardus): Money; fast luck; to draw customers and success in business

Clary Sage: Visions; divination and love
Clover: Fidelity
Cloves: Glamour and fast money; banish a rival; divination; aphrodisiac and to impart vigorous action
Club Moss: Strength; protection and divination
Cocoa Beans (Chocolate): Love and euphoria
Coconut: Purification; protection; good luck and good health. Coconut is the "Tree of Life."
Coffee: Prevent psychic attack and to destroy obstacles
Coltsfoot: Love; money; wealth and divination
Columbine: To reunite lovers; good luck; money and wealth
Comfrey: Money; safe travel and powerful healing
Copal: Love; to attract a very pure love; divination; purification and to attract spirits
Coreopsis: Assertiveness; action and yin energy
Coriander (Cilantro): Romantic love
Corn: Protection; fertility; wealth; good luck and divination
Cotton: Love; good luck and psychic abilities
Couch Grass (Witch Grass): Binding; love and dark arts
Cowslip: Glamour; youthfulness; to increase desirability and to locate hidden treasure
Coxcomb: Protection
Crab's Eye Seeds (Huayruros or Ormusia): To attract good luck and keep away evil.
Crab Apple: Purification
Cramp Bark: Protection and yang energy
Crocus: Visions; increased psychic powers; to promote peace and attract love
Cubeb: Love
Cuckoo Flower: Love and fertility
Cucumber: Healing; fertility and chastity
Cumin: To keep a lover faithful and ward off evil
Curry: Protection
Cyclamen: To forget a lost love; to reinforce a current romance; fertility; lust and protection
Cypress: Protection and longevity

D-F

Daffodil: Romantic love
Daisy: Love; return a lost love and induce flirtatiousness
Damiana: Intensify passion; attract a new love and to cause a lover to return
Damill: Love and lust
Dandelion: Fulfill secret longings; to break hexes; to call spirits; psychic dreams and divination
Date Palm: Fertility and potency
Datura (Jimson Weed): Calm focus; shamanism and to break hexes (Poisonous. Do not ingest.)
Deer's Tongue: Lust and seduction; obtain marriage proposal; for eloquent speech and court cases
Devil Pod (Bat Nut): Protection from evil and an offering to dark spirits
Devil's Bit: Love; lust; protection and exorcism
Devil's Claw: To return lost or stolen items and to repel unwanted guests
Devil's Shoestring: Protection; power; to stop gossip; for gambling; luck and employment
Dill: Love; lust; money; wealth; protection and to break a love spell
Dittany of Crete: To inspire love in another person; manifestations and astral projection
Dock: Money; fertility and healing
Dodder: Love and divination
Dogwood: Love and lust
Dragon's Blood: Love; gambling; confidence and to restore sex drive in men
Dulse (Kelp): Protection; peace; harmony; lust and health
Dutchman's Breeches: Love
Ebony: Protection; power and strength
Echinacea: Health and to strengthen spells
Edelweiss: Protection; invisibility and protection from bullets
Elder Bark: Protection; prosperity; exorcism; sleep; to break hexes and to bring a wealthy love

Elderberry: Healing and visions
Elder Flower: Beauty; to protect property; protection from criminals and law enforcement agents
Elecampane: Love; protection and to increase psychic powers
Elm: Love
Endive: Love and lust
Eryngo (Eryngium): Love; lust; peace and good luck for travelers
Eucalyptus: To ward off evil
Euphorbia: Protection and purification
Evening Primrose (Oenothera biennis): Love and comfort
Eyebright (Euphrasia): Visions; increased mental and psychic powers
False Unicorn: Lust and for protection of mother and child
Fava Beans: To make wishes come true
Fennel Seeds: Protection from witchcraft and law enforcement agents; used in love potions
Fenugreek seed: Prosperity; get a raise; luck with money and wealth
Fern: To prevent hexes; remove evil spirits from the home and ward off robbers
Feverfew: To protect from accidents
Fig: Love; fertility and divination
Figwort: Protection and good health
Five-Finger Grass (Cinquefoil): Money; wealth; to gain favors; gambling and creative inspiration
Flax: Money; protection; beauty; health; mental health and increased psychic powers
Fleabane: Protection; fidelity and exorcism
Foxglove: Protection
Frankincense: Protection; exorcism and increased psychic abilities
Fumitory (Earth Smoke): Exorcism; fast luck and money
Fuzzy Weed: Love and successful hunting

G-L

Galangal (Low John): Money; love; wealth; courage; protection and to drive away bad luck
Gardenia: Love; peace; healing and spirituality
Garlic: Protection of the home; exorcism; lust and to prevent theft
Gentian: Love and strength
Geranium: Love; wealth; power; fertility; courage; protection and good health
Ginger: Money; love; power; protection; gambling; success and restful sleep
Ginger Grass: Healing: an aphrodisiac; causes mood changes
Ginseng: Beauty; increased energy; love; lust; good wishes and protection
Goats Rue: Protection; to make it difficult for an enemy to find you; healing; highly nutritive
Gold of Pleasure (Camelina or False Flax): Wealth; growth; abundance; the oil is used to heal skin
Goldenrod: Love; money and divination
Golden Seal: Money and powerful healing
Ginseng (Wonder of the World): Love; beauty; strength; health; protection and aphrodisiac
Golden Rod: Love and luck
Gorse: Money and protection
Gotu Kola: Strength and meditation
Gourd: Protection of your home or business
Grain: Protection from evil
Grains of Paradise: Love; lust; money; wealth; inspiration and luck
Grapes: Money; fertility and wishes
Grass: Protection and increased psychic powers
Grass of Parnassas: Love and joy
Gravel Root: Job seeking
Ground Ivy: Binding and divination
Groundsel: Good health
Guinea Peppers: Cursing; hexing and dark arts

Gum Arabic (Acacia Senegal): A resin from this particular tree, which is used as a thickening agent
Gum Tragacanth: A binder used in making incense; generally preferred over others for its versatility
Harebell: Prosperity; opening up to the possibility of wealth
Hawthorn: Fertility; fidelity; happiness and good luck fishing
Hazel: Protection; good luck; fertility; to make wishes come true and protection from lightning strike
Heather: Good luck; immortality and protection from violent crime
Heliotrope: Prophetic dreams; visions; prosperity; wealth; invisibility and exorcism
Hemlock: To destroy the sex drive (Caution: This is a deadly poison. Never ingest it in any form.)
Hemp: Meditation; visions; love and relief from anxiety
Henna: Healing
Henbane: To attract love (Poison. Do not ingest)
Hibiscus: Lust; love and divination
Hickory: Court cases; contracts and legal matters
High John the Conqueror (Ipomoea Jalapa): Domination; love; money; gambling and court cases
Holly: Love; money; binding; protection; powerful dreams; protection from lightning strike and evil
Hollyhock: Success; material wealth and riches
Holy Thistle: Purification and breaking hexes
Honeysuckle: Love; happiness; money; prosperity; increased psychic powers and success in business
Hops: Relaxed focus; sleep and divination
Horehound: Exorcism; protection and increased mental powers
Hornbeam: Strength and vitality
Horse Chestnut: Money; healing and increased circulation
Horseradish: Purification and exorcism
Horse Tail (Shavegrass or Colo de Caballo): Beauty; fertility and to charm snakes
Hound's Tongue: To retain wealth and possessions and to quiet barking dogs

Houseleek (Live Forever): Love; protection and good luck
Hyacinth: Love; happiness; protection and peace; good business and court cases
Hydrangea: Protection and hex breaking
Hyssop: Purification; protection and jinx breaking
Indian Paintbrush (Castilleja): Passionate love
Indigo Weed (Baptista): Protection
Iris: Purification and wisdom and to bless infants
Irish Moss: Money; luck and protection
Iron Weed: To control others
Ivy: Binding; protection and healing
Jasmine: Love; heartbreak; money; wealth; inspiration; astral projection; prophetic dreams and court cases
Jezebel Root: Dark arts; hexing; cursing; money; achievement and to attract wealthy customers
Job's Tears: Good luck; gambling and to make wishes come true
Joe-Pye Weed: Love and to inspire respect
Juniper Berries: Love; good luck; wealth; success in business; exorcism and protection from thieves
Karaya: An inexpensive substitute for Gum Tragacanth
Kava Kava: Love and protection
Knotweed: Binding
Kola Nut: Peace and happiness
Lady's Mantle: Love
Lady's Slipper: Protection
Larch: Protection from thieves
Larkspur: Protection and good health
Laurel: Happy marriage
Lavender: Peace; happiness; purification; tranquility and pleasant dreams
Leek: Love; protection and exorcism
Lemon: To evoke longing; for love; purification and immortality
Lemon Balm (Melissa Officinalis): Longevity; love and success
Lemongrass (Cymbopogon): Lust; psychic powers and to repel snakes

Lemon Verbena: Love; luck, purification and to increase the potency of potions
Lettuce: Love; protection from ghosts and divination
Licorice: Love; lust and fidelity
Life Everlasting: Immortality
Lilac: Astral travel
Lily: Protection and to break love spells
Lily of the Valley: Love; happiness; insight and increased mental powers
Lime: Love; happiness and protection
Linden: Love; luck; protection; sleep and immortality
Linseed: Keep a lover faithful
Liverwort (Trefoil): Love and protection
Loosestrife: Peace and protection
Lotus Pods: Break love spells; protection and to open locks
Lovage: Eroticism; to draw love; success and court cases
Love Seed: Love and friendship
Lungwort: Safe air travel; as an offering to spirits of air

M-Q

Mace: Mental and psychic powers
Maguey: Lust
Magnolia: Fidelity and past lives
Mahogany: Protection from lightning strike
Maidenhair: Love and beauty
Male Fern: Love and luck
Mallow: Love and protection
Mandrake(European): Love; wealth; protection; effigy magic and divination. (Poison. Do not ingest)
Maple: Love; lust; money and longevity
Marigold: Protection; increase psychic abilities; legal matters; visions and dreams
Marjoram: Love; happiness; protection and good health
Masterwort: Protection; strength and courage
Mastic (Arabic Gum): Lust; psychic powers and manifestations
May Apple (American Mandrake): Money

Meadow Rue: Divination
Meadow Sweet: Love; happiness; peace and divination
Mesquite: Good health
Milk Thistle: Enrages snakes
Mimosa: Love; protection; visions; past lives and prophetic dreams
Mimulus: Courage
Mint: Aphrodisiac; good luck and to attract helpful spirits
Mistletoe: Love; fertility; breaking hexes; exorcism and a successful hunt (Poison. Do not ingest.)
Molasses: Binding
Molucca Balm: Protection
Monkey Flower: To access higher realms and connect with guardian angels
Moonwort: Love; money and wealth
Moss: Money and good luck
Mugwort: Psychic enhancement; protection; astral projection and prophetic dreams
Mulberry: Protection and strength
Mullein: Love; courage; divination and exorcism
Mustard Seed: Protection from the evil eye; gambling; exorcism and increased mental powers
Myrrh: Purification; exorcism and meditation and to increase the power of potions
Myrtle: Love; fertility; youthfulness; money and peace
Neroli: Love; matrimonial bliss; good luck and to make one more attractive
Nettles: Break up a relationship. exorcism and protection and to inspire lust
Night Jasmine (Cestrum nocturnum, Has No Hana, Hasna Hena): Good luck and gambling
Norfolk Island Pine(Araucaria heterophylla): Protection from evil and poverty
Nutmeg: Money; luck and gambling
Nuts: Love; fertility and prosperity
Oak: Money; good luck; fertility; potency; exorcism; protection and court cases
Oak Moss: Transitions and grounding

Oats: Money
Olive: Lust; fertility; strength; protection and peace
Onion: Money; prophesy; lust; exorcism and to aid in recovery of strength after severe trauma
Orange: Love; luck; money; gambling; insight; meditation; divination and happiness
Orange Blossom: Romantic love; happiness; divination and binding
Oregano: To keep law enforcement agents away and to ward off interfering in-laws
Orchid: Love
Orris Root: Love; protection and divination
Osha Root (Ligusticum Poteri): Purification and good luck
Palmarosa: Good luck and cleansing bad energies
Palo Santo: To remove curses and hexes
Pansy: Love; divination and to bring rain
Parosela: A successful hunt
Parsley: Love; protection; binding and purification
Parsnip: Sex magic for men
Passion Flower: Friendship; peace and to calm nerves
Patchouli: Lust; wealth; fertility and court cases
Paw-paw: Love; protection and revenge
Pea: Love and money
Peach: Love; fertility; longevity; exorcism and fulfillment of wishes
Peat Moss: Protection
Pear: Love and lust
Pecan: Money and steady employment
Pennyroyal: Strength; protection and peace (Caution: The essential oil is poisonous. Do not ingest.)
Peony: Protection and exorcism
Pepper: Protection and exorcism
Peppermint: Purification; exorcism; love; psychic powers; sleep and improved respiration
Pepper Tree: Protection; purification
Periwinkle: Love; lust; money; wealth; protection and fulfillment of wishes

Persimmon: Sex and lust
Pimento: Love
Pimpernel: Protection; especially of emotions and family relations
Pipsissewa (Chimaphila Umbellata): Money; it is used as an incense to call spirits
Pineapple: Luck; money and to keep a lover true
Pine Needles: Money; protection; cleansing; fertility and exorcism
Pistachio: Break love spells
Plantain: Protection; strength and to repel snakes
Plot Weed: Protection
Plumeria (Frangipani): Love and to attract the admiration of others; garnering trust and openness
Poke Root: Courage and breaking hexes
Pomegranate: Fertility; divination; good luck; wishes and wealth
Poppy Seed: Love; wealth; fertility; invisibility and insomnia; used in persuasive love potions
Poplar Bark: Money spells; astral projection and flying potions
Porcupine Plant (Agave Victoriae-reginae): Cursing
Potato: Effigy magic ; youthfulness and healing
Prickly Ash: Love; to break hexes and for safe travel
Primrose: Love; intensifying romance; protection and to compel a person to tell the truth
Prunella (All-heal): Exorcism; healing and to sharpen your powers of observation
Purslane: Love; purification; sleep; protection from psychic attack and to recover money
Quassia: Love
Queen Anne's Lace: Love and to strengthen the bond between two people; used to control fertility
Quina Roja (Cascarilla Colorada): To inspire lust in another person
Quince: Love; protection and happiness

R-Z

Radish: Protection and lust
Ragged Robin: Remove obstacles and purification
Ragweed: Courage
Ragwort: Protection
Raspberry (leaves): Protection; good luck; gambling and love
Rattlesnake Root: Money and protection
Raspberry: Love and protection
Rattlesnake Plantain (Goodyera Oblongifolia): Carried as a good luck charm
Rattle Snake Root: Protection from sudden death and accidents
Rhubarb: Protection and fidelity
Rice: Money; fertility and to bring rain
Rockrose: To expel fear and impart hope
Rose Alba: Love and insight
Rose of Jericho (Anastatica): Money, good luck and prosperity
Rose Geranium: To stop gossip and false accusations and to reverse negativity
Rose Water Lily: Connecting with higher realms
Rose: Love; lust; healing; luck; courage; protection; prophetic dreams and to increase psychic powers
Rosemary: Lust; love; mental power; exorcism; purification and youthfulness and to gain control of a man
Rowan: Protection; power; success; increased psychic powers and healing
Rue: Money drawing; exorcism; increased mental powers; and to break hexes and love spell
Rye: Love and fidelity
Safflower: Purification
Saffron: Love; lust; strength; psychic powers; happiness and to raise winds
Sage: Youth; immortality; wisdom; protection and wishes
Sagebrush: Purification and exorcism

St. John's Wort: Love; strength; happiness and protection from black magic
Salep (Lucky Hand): Money; luck; gambling; employment; protection and safe travel
Sampson Snake (Black Sampson): Love; virility; to enhance masculinity; power and success
Sandalwood: Protection; exorcism; psychic awareness; to increase vibratory rate and astral projection
Sanicle (Saniculus Europaea): Love; to keep a lover; safe travel and healing
Sarsaparilla: Love and wealth
Sassafras: Money and good health
Savory: Increased mental abilities
Scleranthus: To aid in decision making
Scot's Pine: Wisdom
Sea Holly: For achievements and to destroy obstacles
Sea Pink: Auric harmony and connection of vital energies
Sea Rocket: Purity; balance in material matters and regeneration
Senna: Love and to expedite the action of a potion
Sesame: Lust; happiness and wealth
Shallot: Purification
Sheep Sorrel: Purification and healing
Silverweed: Connect to higher planes of awareness
Skullcap: Money; wealth; love; fidelity and peace
Skunk Cabbage: Contracts; court cases and legal matters
Slippery Elm: To stop gossip and slander; to shut someone up
Sloe (Blackthorn or Plum): Black magic; curses and revenge
Smart Weed: Money and wealth
Snakeroot: Luck; money; gambling; protection and health
Snapdragon: Protection and exorcism
Snowdrop: Hope at the darkest hour
Solomon's Seal: Protection and exorcism
Sorrel Wood: Good health
Southern Wood: Love; lust and protection

Spanish Moss: Money and to stop gossip and slander; used in poppet magic
Spearmint: Love and healing; increased mental powers
Spider Wort: Love and binding
Spikenard (Nardostachys Jatmansi): Love; money; protection and strength
Squaw Vine: Fertility and childbirth; to protect children from the evil eye
Squill Root: Money and wealth
Star of Bethlehem: Consolation in times of despair
Stillengia: Increase psychic powers
Stonecrop: Transitions and transformation
Straw: Effigy magic
Straw Flower: Good luck; protection and to prolong the effects of a spell (Poisonous. Do not ingest)
Strawberry: Love; happiness; luck and as an aphrodisiac
Sulfur: Hex breaking; protection and to break someone's control over another person
Sugar Cane: Love; lust and to gain sympathy
Sumac: Leniency and mercy
Sumbul: Love; luck and health; increased psychic powers
Sunflower: Wisdom; fertility; health and wishes
Sweet Grass: To call good spirits
Sweet Orange: Love; divination and money
Sweet Pea: Love; courage; fidelity and friendship
Sycamore: Revitalization
Tamarind: Aphrodisiac
Tamarisk: Protection and exorcism
Tansy: Love; longevity and protection
Tarragon: Confidence; courage; domination; love; passion; strength; protection and to prevent theft
Tea: Wealth; strength and courage
Tea Tree Oil: Protection and purification
Teasle: Healing (Used by alternative practitioners to heal Lyme disease)
Thistle: Strength; protection; exorcism and breaking hexes
Thyme: Used in love spells and divination; sleep; purification; courage; money and psychic abilities

Toadflax: Protection and breaking hexes.
Toadstool: Rain-making (Poisonous)
Tobacco: Purification; spirit communication and hexing
Tomato: Love
Tonka Beans: Good luck in business and courage
Tormentil: Protection; stop slander and gossip
Tuberose: Love and peace
Turmeric: Domination; purification; exorcism; courage and love
Turnip: To end a relationship and protection
Trumpet Weed: Increased male potency
Twitch Grass: To reverse curses and defeat enemies
Unicorn Root: Protection; love and to keep a partner faithful
Uva Ursi (Bearberry): Psychic enhancement and meditation
Valerian: Love; protection; purification and to calm nerves and relax muscles
Vanilla: Love; lust and luck; insight; aphrodisiac and used to increase power of potions
Venus Flytrap: Love and protection
Vervain: Love and fidelity; money; courage; peace and protection
Vetch (Giant): Fidelity
Vetivert (Khus Khus): Love; luck; protection; exorcism and peaceful harmony
Violet: Used in aphrodisiacs; insight; love potions and to get what you want
Walnut: Fertility
Wax Plant: Protection
Wheat (Wheatgrass): Money and fertility
White Pepper: Aphrodisiac
White Peony (Paeonia Lactiflora): Protection and exorcism
White Willow Bark: Love; divination and protection
Wild Cherry Bark: Love and divination
Willowherb (Chamaenerion Angustifolium): Turn authoritarianism to humanitarianism

White Sage: Purification
Willow: Love; divination; protection and conjuring
Winter's Bark: Success
Wintergreen: Luck; strength; protection and breaking hexes
Wisteria: Anointing; meditation; channeling; mental concentration and feminine sexuality
Witch Grass: Love; lust and exorcism
Witch Hazel Bark: Love; fidelity and to heal broken hearts
Wolf's Bane (Aconitum or Monk's Hood): Protection and invisibility (Deadly poison: Do not ingest.)
Witches Burr: To destroy evil and to add power to any potion
Wood Betony: Love and protection
Wood Rose: Good luck and occult powers
Woodruff: Money; protection and success
Wormwood: Love; protection; to call spirits and to cause trouble and strife for enemies
Yarrow: Divination regarding love; understanding of animals; courage and exorcism
Yellow Evening Primrose (Primula Vulgaris): A successful hunt
Yellow Poplar Leaves: Love and binding
Yerba Mate: Love; lust and fidelity
Yerba Santa: Beauty; psychic powers and protection
Yew: Necromancy and to raise the dead
Ylang-ylang: Insight; past lives and lust
Yohimbe: Love and lust
Yucca: Transmutation
Zedoary: Protection; purification; courage; hex breaking and as an aphrodisiac
Zinnia: Love; energy; strength and mental balance

Herbs Classified by Planet

Another method of finding substitutions is to look at other herbs in the same planetary category as the one you wish to find a substitution for. For example, if your missing herb is in the Sun category, look at other herbs under the sign of the Sun for a possible substitution. You will probably have to look at several possibilities and correlate their specific functions before finding the best option.

Herbs are divided by their characteristics as follows:

Sun

Use these herbs in potions involving success, fame, wisdom, family, authority figures and court cases.

Acacia, Agave, Almond, Angelica, Ash Tree, Bay, Benzoin, Blueweed (Echium Vulgare), Bergamot, Bromeliad, Burnet, Butterbur, Chamomile, Celandine, Centaury, Cinnamon, Dragonroot (Poisonous), Eyebright, Frankincense, Galangal (Low John), Grapefruit, Heart Trefoil, Heliotrope, High John, Honeywort, Jerusalem Artichoke, Juniper, Laurel, Lemon, Life Everlasting, Lime, Lovage, Marigold, Mayweed, Mistletoe, Olibanum, Olive, Orange, Peony, Pimpernel, Rice, Rosemary, Rue, Saffron, Saint Joan's Wort, Saint John's Wort, Saxifrage, Spelt, Sundew, Sunflower, Tormentil, Vine, Walnut and Water Pimpernel

Moon

Use these herbs in potions involving the mind, dreams, divination, the home, meditation, planting and harvesting.

Acanthus, (Bear's Breech), Adder's Tongue, Aloe, Aloe Vera, Anise Seed, Anise, Ash, Buchu, Cabbage, Calamus, Camphor, Chickweed, Christ's Eye (Wild Clary), Clary Sage, Cleavers, Coconut, Coriander, Cucumber, Dog Rose, Dogs Tooth Violet, Dogwood, Duckweed, Dwarf Rocket Cress, Flag, Flaverel, Fleur-de-lis, French Mercury, Gardenia, Ginger, Grape, Great Burnet Saxifrage, Guaran (Guar Gum), Holly, Iris, Jasmine, Lemon, Lemon Balm (Melissa Officinalis), Lettuce, Lily, Moonwort, Orpine, Orris Root, Pearl Trefoil, Poppy, Privent, Pumpkin, Purslane, Queen Elizabeth Root, Rose (White and Wild), Rowan, Sea Coleworts, Sedum, Sesame Seeds, Serpent's Tongue, Star Anise, Stonecrop, Turnip, Watercress, Water Lily, Willow, Wintergreen and Yellow Flag

Mercury

Use these herbs in potions involving higher learning, occult studies, business, the arts, sales, writing, short trips and deceptions.

Agaric, Azaleas, Balsam, Bayberry, Bittersweet, Buckwheat, Calamint, Caraway, Carrots, Cascara, Cassia, Cedar, Celery, Cinquefoil (Five Finger Grass), Coffee, Crouch Grass (Quick Grass), Dill, Elecampane, Elfwort, Fennel, Fenugreek, Fern, Five Leaf Grass, Flax, Gentian, Goat's Rue, Grape, Hare's Foot, Hazel Nut, Henry (Good King Henry), Honeysuckle, Honeywort, Horehound, Hounds-tongue, Jacob's Ladder, Lady's Slipper, Lavender, Lily of the Valley, Licorice, Mace, Maidenhair Fern, Mace Mandrake, Marjoram, Mastic, Meadowsweet, Mulberry, Mushrooms, Myrtle, Parsley, Parsnips, Pellitory, Pomegranate, Sassafras, Savory, Scabious, Sledge, Smallage (Wild Celery), Senna, Southernwood, Spruge, Starwort, Trefoil, Tea, Valerian, Wisteria, Woody Nightshade and Wormwood

Venus

Use these herbs in potions involving love, friendship, social situations, weddings, engagements, romance and communications with women.

Alder (common and black), Alkanet, Ambrette (Musk Seed), Apple Blossom, Apricot, Balm of Gilead, Beans, Bedstraw, Bergamot, Birch, Birth Root (Beth Root), Bishops' Weed, Blackberry, Bloodroot, Blue Flag, Boneset, Buckwheat, Bugle, Burdock, Cardamom, Catnip, Celery, Cherry Tree, Chick-pea, Clover, Coltsfoot, Columbines, Cornflower, Cowslip, Daffodil, Daisy, Dittany of Crete, Dropwort, Dwarf Elder, Elder, Eryngo, Feverfew, Figwort, Flea Bean, Foxglove, Gardenia, Goldenrod, Golden Seal, Gooseberry, Gosmore, Groundsel, Heather, Herb True-Love, Hibiscus, Hollyhock, Jewelweed, Kava-Kava, Ladies Mantle, Lemon, Lemon Balm, Lemongrass, Lentil, Mallow, Marshmallow, Mint, Moneywort, Motherwort, Mugwort, Orach, Orchid, Peach, Pear, Pennyroyal, Peppermint, Periwinkle, Plantain, Plum, Poley, Primrose, Ragweed, Rampion, Raspberry, Red Clover, Red Fitchling (Cock's Head), Rose (Red), Rose Geranium, Rose Hips, Sage, Sanicle (Saniculus), Sea Blites, Self-Heal, Silverweed, Skirret, Soapwort, Sorrel, Speedwell, Strawberry, Sycamore, Tansy, Teasel, Thyme, Verbena, Vervain, Violet, Wheat, Wood Sage and Yarrow

Mars

Use these herbs in potions involving passion, aggression, courage, adventure, success in military actions, success in law suits, conflicts and sports.

Acacias, Adam and Eve Root (Arum Maculatum), Agave, All-Heal, Aloe, Anemone, Barberry, Basil, Bearberry, Beech, Benzoin, Black Pepper, Blessed Thistle (Holy Thistle), Briony, Broom, Buttercup (Crowfoot), Byronia, Cashew, Cayenne, Cedar, Chives, Citronella, Coriander (Cilantro), Cotton Thistle (Onopordum Acanthium), Cubeb (Piper Cubeba), Cumin, Curry, Daffodil, Dogwood, Dragon's Blood Reeds, Felwort, Fern (Male), Faired, Flax (Linseed), Galangal (Low John), Garlic, Gentian, Germander (Poisonous), Goat's Thorn, Gorse (Furze), Ground Pine, Gum Mastic, Gum Thistle, Hawthorn, Honeysuckle, Hops, Horseradish, Horse Tongue (Hart's Tongue), Hyssop, Juniper, Kidney-Leaved Sower Weed, Lady's Thumb (Polygonum Persicaria), Leeks, Loosestrife, Lupine (Lupinus Albus), Madder Root, Marjoram, Masterwort, Mastic Herb, Mustard, Nettles, Onion, Orchid Root, Paprika, Parsley, Peppers, Pilewort, Pine, Plantain, Rhubarb, Rocket, Rue, Salep (Lucky Hand), Saltwort, Samphire (Salicornia Europaea), Sanicle, Sarsaparilla, Savine, Shepherd's Rod, Sloe, Snapdragon, Solomon's Seal, Spurge, Squill (Poisonous), Tarragon, Tobacco, Toothwort (Bulbiferous), Turmeric, Uva-Ursi, Wintercress (St. Barbara's Herb), Woodruff, Wormseed, Wormwood and Zedoary

Jupiter

Use these herbs in potions involving abundance, prosperity, growth, expansion, investments, good luck, money spells, settling disputes and blessings.

Agrimony, Alfalfa, Arrowroot, Avens, Balm, Betony, Bilberry, Bladderwrack, Bodhi, Borage, Box, Briar Rose, Cardamom, Chervil, Chestnut, Cicely, Cinquefoil, Costmary, Couch Grass (Twitch, Quack Grass or Dog Grass), Currant, Dandelion, Devil's Claw, Dock, Eglantine, Endive, Fig, Fir Tree, Five Leaf Grass, Goat's Beard, Gold of Pleasure (Camelina Sativa) or False Flax), Golden Samphire (Limbarda Crithmoides), Hare's Ear, Hart's Tongue, Henna, Hyssop, Jasmine, Lime, Houseleek (Live Forever), Liverwort, Lungwort, Magnolia, Maple, Meadowsweet, Milkweed, Mistletoe, Moneywort, Moss (Sphagnum), Myrrh, Oak, Ox Tongue (Picris), Pinks, Pleurisy Root, Rose Hips, Sage, Sandalwood, Spinach, Succory, Sumac, Swallow Wort, Swamp Milkweed, Sweet Briar, Thorn Apple, Thorough Wax and Whitlow Grass

Saturn

Use these herbs in potions involving binding, restricting, decreasing, contracts, legal matters, discipline, chronic illnesses, cursing, hexing, hex breaking, revenge, reversal spells and the dark arts.

Aconite, Ambrette (Musk Seed), Amaranthus, Arnica, Asafoetida, Barley, Beech Tree, Beet, Belladonna, Bindweed, Birdsfoot, Bistort (Snake Weed), Black Fungus (Jew's Ear Mushroom), Black Hellebore, Blackthorn Berries (Sloe), Bluebell, Boneset, Buck's Horn Plantain, Buckthorn, Campion, Clematis, Comfrey, Cornflower, Cramp Bark, Crosswort, Cypress, Dodder, Dogs Grass, Elm, Fern, Flea Wort, Fumitory, Gall Oak, Gladiolus, Goat Herb, Hawk Weed, Heart's Ease, Hemlock (Poisonous), Hemp, Henbane, Holly, Horsetail (Shavegrass), Irish Moss, Ivy, Juniper, Knapweed, Knapwort, Knot Grass, Laurel, Morning Glory (Bind Weed), Meadow Saffron, Medlar, Moss, Mullein, Musk, Navelwort (Umbilicus), Pansies, Paris Quadrifolia (Herb Paris or True-lover's Knot), Poke, Poplar, Poppy, Queen's Delight (Stillingia Sylvatica), Quince, Root of Scarcity (Mangel Wurzel, a type of Beet Root), Safflower, Sciatica Wort (Sciatica Grass), Service Tree, Shepherd's Purse, Skullcap, Solomon's Seal, Spikenard, Tamarisk, Thorough Leaf, Thrift, Tutsan (Park Leaves), Virginia Creeper, Water Violet, Willow, Witch Hazel, Woad (Glastum), Wolf's Bane and Yew

Herbs Classified by Zodiac Signs

You can, also, find substitutions by looking for another herb in the same zodiac sign as the original. Herbs are divided by their zodiacal characteristics as follows:

Aries
Use these herbs in potions involving passion, health, vitality, appearance and quick action.

Anemone, Betony, Blackberry, Blessed Thistles, Broom, Burnet, Capers, Cayenne Pepper, Cinnamon, Cypress, Cowslip, Garlic, Gentian, Geranium, Hawthorn, Honeysuckle, Hops, Horseradish, Mustard, Nettles, Pine Needles, Rosemary, Sweet Pea, Tobacco, Vanilla, Wormwood

Taurus
Use these herbs in potions involving stability, money, possessions acquired by marriage or inheritance, banking, finances and the need for tenacity.

Apple Blossom, Bearberry, Clover, Cloves, Coltsfoot, Cumin, Daisy (Bellis Perennis), Musk, Rose, Carnation, Figwort, Goldenrod, Honeysuckle, Jasmine, Lovage, Plantain, Primrose, Sage, Sorrel, Spearmint, Strawberry, Thyme, Vervain and Mallow

Gemini

Use these herbs in potions involving communications, eloquence, the arts, sales, study and travel.

Balm, Bayberry, Bittersweet, Caraway, Flax, Jasmine, Lavender, Marjoram, Mastic Resin, Rose (Yellow), Sandalwood, Skullcap, Marjoram, Parsley, Gladiolus and Orchid

Cancer

Use these herbs in potions involving leadership, protection, property, the home and success.

Adder's Tongue, Agrimony, Aloe, Balm of Gilead, Bay Leaves, Buckbean, Calamus, Cedar, Chickweed, Cinnamon, Daisy, Devil's Claw, Eucalyptus, Honeysuckle, Hyacinth, Larkspur, Myrtle, Nocturnal Flowers, Poppy, Saxifrage, Serpent's Tongue, Sundew, Lotus, Tarragon, Verbena and Water Lily

Leo

Use these herbs in potions involving the family, success in relationships, children, gambling and joy.

Bay Tree, Calendula, Camphor, Cassia, Chamomile, Clove, Eyebright, Frankincense, Golden Rod, Great Celandine, Eyebright, Goat's Rue, Peppermint, Red Sandalwood, Rosemary, Rue, Saffron, Sunflower, Walnut

Virgo

Use these herbs in potions involving a need for assistance or analysis of a situation, health, diet, exercise and pets.

Aster, Cardamom, Cornflower, Citron, Mace, Caraway Seed, Endive, Fennel, Horehound, Lavender, Licorice, Lily, Male Fern, Marjoram, Snowdrop, Morning Glory, Myrrh, Narcissus, Petunias, Skullcap, Tarragon, Violet and Verbena

Libra

Use these herbs in potions involving fairness, justice, contracts, legal matters, marriages and business partnerships.

Aloe, Angelica, Bearberry, Burdock, Calendula, Cayenne, Golden Rod, Mint, Pennyroyal, Periwinkle, Primrose, Vervain, Pennyroyal, Rose, Sandalwood, Satinwood, Thyme and Violet

Scorpio

Use these herbs in potions involving sex, death, drugs, past lives, inheritances, surgery and investments.

Aloes, Anemone, Basil, Catnip, Chrysanthemum, Cypress, Dogwood, Horehound, Horseradish, Leek, Little Celandine, Nettles, Pine, Rosemary, Sasparilla, Wormwood, Vanilla, Witch Hazel and Yucca

Sagittarius

Use these herbs in potions involving long-distance travel, short-term relationships, foreign language studies, foreign travel, books, publishing, religion and philosophy.

Agrimony, Anise, Aster, Balsam, Balm, Bilberry, Burdock, Chicory, Cinnamon, Cinquefoil (Five Finger Grass), Clove, Daffodil, Dandelion, Dock, Goat's Beard, Moss, Narcissus, Nutmeg, Oak bark, Pimpernel, Red Clover, Saffron and Sage

Capricorn

Use these herbs in potions involving ambitions, careers, obtaining authority or high status, getting and maintaining control of a situation, prestige and reputation.

Carnation, Comfrey, Dandelion, Flax, Frankincense, Hemlock, Hemp, Henbane, Horsetail, Iceland Moss, Knapweed, Shepherd's Purse, Slippery Elm, Sorrel, Thistle, Thyme and Vetivert

Aquarius

Use these herbs in potions involving community, volunteer work, society, activism, group activities and strong emotions.

Absinthe, Barley, Buttercup, Comfrey, Chile Peppers, Daffodil, Fennel, Flax, Iceland Moss, Myrrh, Pepperwort, Pine, Poppy, Sciaticawort, Southernwood, Valerian and Violets.

Pisces

Use these herbs in potions involving secrets, hospitals, prisons, dreams, fears and other negative emotions.

Balsam, Birthwort, Carnation, Cinquefoil, Clove, Dock, Dogwood, Irish Moss, Lilac, Lilies, Lime, Moss, Nutmeg, Pellitory, Sage Seaweeds, Sea Moss, Succory and Water Plants

Quick Color Guide

Colors radiate their own unique vibrational harmonies that can influence a potion. Consider the following as a general guideline in relation to the purpose of stones, candles or other items used in the construction of your formulas. The color on the left corresponds with the characteristics on the right.

Black: Protection; revenge; dark arts
Blue: (Jupiter) Occult knowledge; psychic abilities; protection; stability and commitment
Brown: Legal matters; court cases and contracts
Gold: (Sun) Domination; success in career; victory in war; great wealthy; imparts the energy of the sun

Green: (Venus) Money; prosperity; wealth abundance; good fortune; material success
Orange: (Mercury) Career and legal matters; imparts cleansing energy.
Pink: Friendship; kindness; romance and affection; imparts gentle energy

Purple: (Saturn) Higher intuition; spiritualism; psychic abilities; peace; idealism; selflessness
Red: (Mercury) Passion; energy; strength; physical health; courage and sexual potency; imparts vigorous energy
Silver: (Moon) Clairvoyance; intuition; inspiration; astral travel; dreams; divination; money; imparts the energy of the moon
White: Purity; peace and protection. It is considered an all-purpose color whenever other colors are not available
Yellow: (Earth) Education; thought; intellectual pursuits; material wealth; memory and inspiration

In Hoodoo, washes and other preparations are sometimes dyed based on their purpose, as follows:

Blue: Protection and friendship
Red: Luck, power and protection
Yellow: Money

Part II
The Potions

4 INKS OF ART

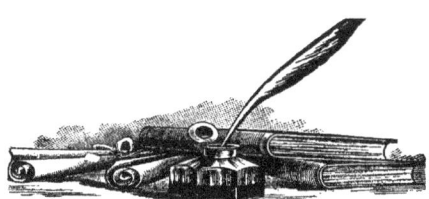

Inks of Art are used for recording spells in magical journals or Books of Shadows and for the casting of spells. In any spell where you are required to write a request, a petition or make a sigil, you may use Inks of Art and write with a calligraphy pen or sharpened quill feather.

In these formulas, Gum Arabic, also called Acacia Gum, is used as a thickening agent. It is a substance extracted from the particular species of Acacia tree called Acacia Senegal.

Always powder the ingredients used in the creation of your inks very finely. Macerate and blend the formula until it is smooth.

Adjust the thickness by the amount of Gum Arabic used. It can be thinned with a formula of two parts water and one part alcohol. Always, begin with a very tiny amount before adding more to avoid over thickening the ink.

Bat's Blood Ink
To bind or curse

2/3 oz. of Water
1/3 oz. of Alcohol
A dash of powdered Gum Arabic
A dash of powdered Myrrh
A dash of powdered Cinnamon
A few drops of black food dye. (Or, make it dark red with a few drops of red and black.)

Dove's Blood Ink
For love

2/3 oz. of Water
1/3 oz. of Alcohol
A dash of powdered Gum Arabic
A dash of powdered Dragon's Blood
3 drops of Rose Geranium
A few drops of red food dye

Dragon's Blood Ink
For increased power

2/3 oz. of Water
1/3 oz. of Alcohol
A dash of powdered Gum Arabic
A dash of powdered Dragon's Blood
A few drops of red food dye

Dragon's Blood adds power to any potion. Dragon's Blood Ink formula is used in spells and petitions for drawing money, power strength and protection. It is a very versatile formula that has a low, nearly physical vibrational harmony, which aids in manifesting quick results.

Jupiter Ink
Spells for success, to enhance psychic abilities and for keeping records in your Book of Shadows

2/3 oz. of Water
1/3 oz. of Alcohol
A dash of powdered Gum Arabic
A dash of Nutmeg
5 to 10 drops of Bergamot oil
A few drops of blue food dye

Venus Ink
For love and fertility

To make Venus Ink, use the same formula given for Dove's Blood above, but dye the ink green instead of red.

Pact Ink

The following formula is for Pact Ink, which is used when making agreements with demonic entities according to the *Grimoirum Verum*. Some clarifications have been made to this formula for the modern reader. (You may find the original grimoire on-line. Use the search terms: *Grimoirum Verum* Public Domain.)

10 oz. Gall nuts (The sap of gall nuts has long been a source for inks. They are the hard kernels formed when animals bore into trees to lay their eggs. Primarily, gall nuts from oak trees are used. Gall nuts can be purchased on-line.)
3 oz. Roman Vitriol (Blue stones available from Hoodoo shops and Botanicas) or Green Copperas (Copper Sulfate)
3 oz. Gum Arabic

Caution: Roman Vitriol or Copper Sulfate is a highly corrosive substance that poses a deadly threat to humans and other creatures if even very tiny amounts are ingested. Handle it with great care and dispose of it properly.

Poke Root Ink

Traditionally, the juice of fresh, crushed Poke Root Berries is used as ink for making pacts and recording spells.

General Instructions for Ink Formulas

Excluding the dye, combine the ingredients in a bottle and allow the resin to dissolve a little bit. Then, blend it in a mortar and pestle until it is smooth. Then, add the dye.

These formulas call for food dye, but as recently as 100 years ago Red Carmen, a natural red substance still used as a fabric dye, was used. Red Carmen is relatively inexpensive and can be purchased online. Other substances were used as dyes in ink black more than a century ago, but they are now deemed toxic and are difficult to obtain.

When creating inks or any other dyed potions, use a stainless steel vessel or one made of a kind of material that won't become stained by this process. Combine all other ingredients in the potion and mix them thoroughly before adding the dye to a smaller portion. Dye a small amount first, then continue adding dye until the ink is a color you are pleased with.

Carefully pour the freshly made ink into a short bottle or very small jar with a tightly fitting lid. Cap the bottle tightly and store it in a cool, dark place until you're ready to use it.

Historically, blood alone has been used as ink or added to ink for potency and to retain the impressions the maker or user imbues the formula with by way of focused concentration. Menstrual blood is traditionally added, especially in formulas pertaining to love or domination of another person. A few drops of semen may, also, be used to add a fiery energy to the formula. It is suggested that you only use these very personal items in formulas you plan to use for yourself. If you make the formula for another person, you may advise the user that it can be enhanced in this way.

Caution: Always take care not to get ink on your clothes, carpeting or other surfaces that could be stained.

Sophia diGregorio

5 CONVERSION OF OIL, INCENSE, POWDER AND WASH FORMULAS

Some of the formulas given here can be converted from one form to another. For example, essential oils of herbs used in an oil formula can be used as dry herbs in that formula. They may be pulverized to make a powder or incense. Or, they may be boiled to make a wash.

Powder formulas can be converted to oil formulas by using essential oils in place of dry ingredients or by steeping the dried herbs in an oil base.

Specifically, you can produce an oil in the following ways:

(1) Combine the powdered form of the herb with a base oil, such as Almond, Safflower or Sunflower, cover the herb in a glass jar completely, then about two times more so that 1/2 to 1/3 of the jar is herbs and the other 1/2 to 2/3 is oil. Allow this to sit for, at least, two weeks in a warm place. Shake the jar twice per day. Then, strain the oil into a bottle using cheesecloth or a strainer and label it accordingly. This method produces an oil infusion.

(2) Combine a few drops of each essential oil of the herb in

the recipe into a base of approximately two ounces of Almond, Safflower or Sunflower oil.

(3) Use a combination of these methods.

Almond is frequently given as the base oil in formulas in this book because it is known for its power and speed of action, but you may substitute any base oil you prefer. Almond oil speeds the action of a potion, but in some cases, you may want to substitute coconut oil, which brings purification, healing and protection to the potion. In other cases, olive oil may be preferred, especially where the potions have Biblical associations or purification, peace and tranquility are desired.

You may use other base oils, either based on the characteristics given in the herb list in a previous chapter or simply on the basis of availability. For example, in a love formula, you might choose to use Apricot oil instead of Almond oil. Or, you may use half and half to provide both power and love energy to the potion.

Often, more exotic ingredients are unnecessarily expensive or difficult to find. In these cases, it makes sense to use what we already have in our cupboards or what is most available to use at a local store.

Powder formulas given here can be used as loose incense, either used alone or when they are burned on a piece of charcoal. Several drops of an oil formula can be applied to a charcoal, as well, and used as an incense. Always use an appropriate charcoal burner on a surface such as ceramic tile or brick that can absorb heat because charcoal becomes extremely hot. Always follow the directions on your charcoal incense burner package. Lighting loose incense without charcoal will still produce heat, flames and smoke, so take similar precautions.

Powders are employed in spells in different ways. They are sprinkled on the object that represents the situation or person you want to influence; they are sprinkled in a specific place, such as your home or business, where you want to gain influence; or blown into the outside air to disseminate their influence upon the winds. The degree to which you pulverize powder remedies may vary according to your intended use. For many spell formulas a fine powder is not necessary, but for sprinkling or blowing a finer consistency is required. You may, also, thin the powder with a little cornstarch, talc or similar fine powdery substance.

Just as with oil formulas, oils may sometimes be substituted in cases where you cannot easily obtain the dried form of the herb.

To create house washes using any of these recipes, combine the herbs and boil them. Then, strain and use the liquid as a wash to scrub the floors, walls, porches and sidewalks of your home or business. House washes are commonly used to keep bad spirits away, invite kindly ones and to bring influences such as love, money and harmony into your house or place of business.

To make a ritual bath, place several drops of an oil formula in your bath water. Ritual baths are commonly performed before spells to cleanse the body of negative energies, which might exert an unwanted influence on the proceedings. They are, also, used in spells.

Both baths and washes have a similar purpose, which is to rid an area of adversarial vibrations and impart harmonious or desirable ones. Wash formulas can, also, be used as baths. Always keep your personal skin sensitivities or allergies in mind and exclude or replace ingredients that you think might cause an adverse reaction.

Another method of making a wash suitable for either home and business or bathing your body is to combine the desired oil with a little unscented liquid Castille soap. Dilute this soap to make wash suitable for washing virtually any surface that can be cleaned.

You can, also, make bath salts from these herb and oil formulas. To make bath salts combine sea salt with powder or essential oil and crush the mixture using a mortar and pestle.

Sophia diGregorio

6 OILS

Magical oils are employed in a variety of ways. They are used to anoint petitions, papers other objects used in a spell and people. They can be used to exorcise spirits or to invite them in. They are applied to your clothes, used to dress mojo bags (medicine bags) and as dressings for candles. In some cases, oils can be worn on the skin as a fragrance.

When selecting oils for your formulas, avoid fragrance oils. These are synthetics, which sometimes contain toxic chemicals and do not possess the same vibration as natural essential oils extracted from plants.

When you purchase essential oils, try to get the highest grade of oils you can find, which are either food grade or therapeutic. Some high-quality essential oils can be very expensive. If you order oils on-line, ask the seller to send samples of the product before you purchase larger quantities.

Most brands of essential oils are diluted with Jojoba oil, which is another essential oil that is stable and relatively long-lasting. This entitles the manufacturer to declare that their product is 100% essential oil, despite the fact that their product may be very diluted. If you are using a very diluted essential oil, you may have to use more drops than these formulas suggest. Experience and your own olfactory senses will soon become your guide as you experiment with different manufacturers' products.

Take care applying certain oils to your skin, particularly if you are sensitive or prone to allergies. For example, Cinnamon oil may burn your skin if it is not well-diluted with a carrier oil. Certain oils, especially citrus oils, applied to the skin can cause changes in coloration if skin is exposed to sunlight. If you are pregnant or nursing, you should take care not to apply these oils to your skin. Essential oils should never be applied to infants, toddlers or cats.

Sometimes a formula calls for an herbal oil that is not commonly available as an essential oil. This is the case with some roots like High John the Conqueror and flower essences like Lily of the Valley. In cases where you cannot obtain the essential oil, make an oil infusion by placing one part of dried, crushed or powdered herb in one or two parts of base oil and allowing it to macerate for, at least, two weeks before straining and bottling it.

Other substitutes for essential oils in these formulas are absolutes and extracts or tinctures. Absolutes are similar to essential oils, but the essence of the herb is extracted into an organic solvent. Extracts are similar to absolutes. Absolutes and extracts can be stronger than essential oils, so adjust the formula according to their strength relative to the strength of the essential oils used in the formula. Always blend your potions well and shake the bottle before using them.

Place your finished potions in sealed bottles or jars. Tinted glass bottles are best and plastic should be avoided. Label them for future use and store them at a low temperature out of direct sunlight. Stored properly, oil formulas should last, at least, two years. Some essential oils have a much longer shelf life than others.

Abramelin Oil No. 1
To increase occult powers; used in ceremonial magic

This formula is derived from the original one given in the Medieval grimoire, The Book of Abramelin, by Abraham the Jew using the Peter Hammer 1725 German translation, which calls for simply "tree oil," without specifying a particular tree.[3] It is commonly assumed that the original oil used was from the Olive tree because it is common in the region. What seems to be most important is the proportions of Cinnamon and Calamus in relation to the Myrrh and Cassia in the formula, which is reflected here.

1/2 Almond oil
2 T. Cinnamon
2 T. Calamus
1 T. Myrrh
1 T. Cassia Leaf

Mix and pulverize the dry ingredients. Add them to the oil. Place the jar in a warm place out of direct sunlight for two weeks. Strain and bottle.

Abramelin Oil No. 2

The following formula is a slight variation on the original above. It can be made using a combination of essential oils, as well, keeping similar ratios. It is based on the work of MacGregor Mathers and others. Mathers' variation used only the Cinnamon, Galangal and Myrrh in the ratios relative to one another as shown below. His formula, also, used Olive oil, specifically. The use of Almond oil in this formula and throughout this book is an American Hoodoo influence.

1 cup Almond oil
1 T. Calamus
1 T. Cassia
4 T. Cinnamon
1 T. Galangal
2 T. Myrrh

Mix and pulverize the dry ingredients. Add them to the oil. Place the jar in a warm place out of direct sunlight for two weeks. Strain and bottle.

Admiration Oil

Make and wear the following formula to attract the admiration of others. It is used not only to attract romantic admiration, but to garner the approval of others.

1/2 cup Almond oil
7 drops Jasmine oil
3 drops Ylang-ylang oil
3 drops Rose oil
3 drops Cowslip oil

Blend these ingredients together in a bottle and leave them in the moonlight.

All Purpose Oil
Similar to Hoodoo traditional Special Oil No. 20 or Wick Oil; gives power to any spell or petition

1/4 cup Olive oil
Pinch of Sea Salt (optional)

Olive oil is traditionally used in this formula. Sometimes it is used alone or it may be combined with a pinch of sea salt or kosher salt. Place the oil and optional salt in a jar or bottle. Place your left hand, palm downward over the top of it. Then, place your right hand on top of the left in a similar fashion to form a cross. Project your body's electro-magnetic energy into the oil and pronounce the words of Psalm 23, as follows:

"The Lord is my shepherd; I shall not want. He maketh me to lie down in green pastures. He leadeth me beside the still waters. He restoreth my soul. He leadeth me in the paths of righteousness for his name's sake. Yea, though I walk through the valley of the shadow of death, I will fear no evil, for thou art with me. Thy rod and thy staff they comfort me. Thou preparest a table before me in the presence of mine enemies. Thou anointest my head with oil. My cup runneth over. Surely goodness and mercy shall follow me all the days of my life and I will dwell in the house of the Lord forever. Amen."

Then, point your index finger and your middle finger at the bottle of oil and salt say, "In the name of the Father, the Son and the Holy Ghost." Draw a cross in the air with your two fingers over the top of the jar as you pronounce each of the three names of the trinity.

All Saints Oil

In a base of two cups of Almond, Olive, Safflower or Sunflower oil combine the following:

7 drops White Peony (paeonia lactiflora)
3 drops Cinnamon
3 drops Patchouli
3 drops Vanilla
7 drops Lavender
3 drops Gardenia
3 drops Vetivert

This oil attracts good spirits, enhances your psychic abilities and helps you connect with the spirit realm. Apply this oil as a dressing to candles, to your body or add several drops of oil to your bath water.

Altar Oil
Used to anoint your altar and ritual items

1/4 cup Almond oil
4 drops Frankincense oil
2 drops Myrrh oil
1 drop Cedar oil

Anointing Oil

1/4 cup Almond oil
5 drops Sandalwood oil
3 drops Cedar oil
2 drops Frankincense oil

As You Please Oil
Inspires kindness and generosity toward you

1/2 cup Almond oil
7 drops Ambergris or Ambrette
7 drops Bergamot
7 drops Calamus
7 drops Orange Blossom
7 drops Mint

Astral Projection Oil
To aid in meditation and astral projection

1/2 cup Hemp oil
7 drops Frankincense
7 drops Jasmine
7 drops Myrrh
7 drops Sandalwood

Attract a Lover Oil

1/4 cup Almond oil
1 tsp. Blue Cohosh
1 tsp. Cinnamon
1 tsp. Lemon Verbena
1 tsp. Patchouli
1 tsp. Rose petals
1 tsp. Vetivert
A Lodestone

Combine approximate amounts of the above herbs. Allow to remain in a warm place for two weeks before straining. Add a lodestone to the master bottle.

Attract a Woman Oil

1/2 cup Almond oil
3 drops Allspice oil
6 drops Ambergris oil
6 drops Ambrette oil
3 drops Carnation oil
6 drops Cinnamon oil
3 drops Patchouli oil

Attraction Oil
To attract anything you desire

1/2 cup Almond oil
7 drops Rose oil
3 drops Lavender oil
3 drops Vanilla oil
3 drops Sandalwood oil

Attraction Oil No. 2
Traditional Hoodoo Formula

Holy Oil
2 Lodestones

Obtain Holy Oil from a Catholic Church or make your own using the formula for All Purpose Oil given above. Place the oil in a bottle together with two lodestones. This formula is derived from information obtained by The Georgia Writer's Project and recorded in the book, *Drums and Shadows*, published in 1940.[4]

Banishing Oil
To drive away unwholesome energies or unwanted persons

1/4 cup Almond oil
8 drops Patchouli
5 drops Cedar oil
3 drops Clove oil
3 drops Dragon's Blood oil
Small piece of Jet or Black Obsidian in the master bottle.

Bat's Blood Oil
To hex or curse

1/4 cup Almond oil
1 tsp. Dragon's Blood
1 tsp. Red Pepper
Pinch of Black Pepper
Jezebel root in the master bottle

Bend Over Oil
Curse reversal, hex breaking, commanding

Almond oil
Allspice
Bergamot
Calamus root
Cinnamon
Frankincense
Honeysuckle blossoms
Licorice root
Vetivert
White Rose petals

To make the oil, combine the above powdered herbs in approximately equal parts in a jar, cover it twice over with Almond oil. Keep it in a warm place for two weeks, shaking it once or twice per day. Strain and bottle it. For extra power, add a few drops of Van Van Oil (Formula is below).

Black Cat Oil
For good luck and to reverse bad luck

1/2 cup Almond oil
1 T. Angelica root
1 T. St. John's Wort
1 T. Rose Geranium
2 T. Solomon's Seal
2 T. Chamomile
Pinch of Sea Salt

Place the above ingredients into a jar with a lid. Allow the jar to sit in a warm place, out of direct sunlight for a couple of weeks. Shake the jar once or twice per day. After, at least, two weeks, strain the liquid into a bottle.

Rub a drop or two of this oil on your hands before gambling.

Binding Oil

1/4 cup Almond oil
1 tsp. Byrony
1 tsp. Couch Grass (Witch Grass)
1 tsp. Devil's Shoestring
1 tsp. Knotweed
1 tsp. Cobwebs (Spider's Web)

Blessed Anointing Oil

Say a prayer, addressing the deity of your choice over plain Olive oil, similar to the procedure for All Purpose Oil, above.

Come to Me Oil

1/2 cup Almond oil
3 drops Rose oil
3 drops Jasmine oil
3 drops Bergamot oil
7 drops Damiana oil

Come to Me Now Oil
A more expedient version of the previous formula

1/2 cup Almond oil
3 drops Cinnamon oil
3 drops Ambergris oil
2 drops Ylang-ylang oil
2 drops Vanilla oil
Pinch of Orris Root Powder

Confusion Oil
To throw an enemy into a state of bewilderment

1/2 cup Almond oil
3 drops Patchouli oil
3 drops Capsicum (This is very spicy pepper, take caution with eyes, skin and inhalation)
3 drops Celandine oil
Pinch of dried Black Pepper
Pinch of dried Red Pepper
Pinch of Black Mustard Seeds
Pinch of Poppy Seeds
1 tsp. Graveyard Dirt (Gathered at midnight during a waning moon, preferably from the grave of murder.)

Macerate these ingredients and store the bottle in a dark place until you're ready to use it.

Consecration Oil
Use this oil to consecrate an altar and magical tools

1/4 cup Almond oil
10 drops Frankincense oil
10 drops Myrrh oil
5 drops Cinnamon oil
A Bay leaf

Contra la Ley Oil
To keep cops and other law enforcement agents away

Combine the following in a jar with a lid:

1 cup Almond oil
2 T. Anise
2 T. Palo Espanta Policia ("Scare Away Police" sticks are available at online botanicas)
2 T. Celandine (or 10 drops of oil)
1 T. Ginger root (or 10 drops of oil)
1 T. Dragon's blood resin
1 T. Oregano (or 10 drops of oil)
Pinch of Licorice sticks
1 tsp. Deer Horn powder
1 tsp. of Vitamin E oil (optional, as a preservative)

Place the lid on the jar and put it a warm place. Shake it twice per day for two weeks. Then, strain the liquid. Bottle it and store it in in a cool, dark place. Palo Espanta Policia is a critical ingredient in the original formula.

Contra la Ley No. 2

1/4 cup Almond oil
1 tsp. Celandine
1/4 tsp. Fennel
1 T. Licorice root
1 tsp. Oregano
1 tsp. Tansy
1/4 tsp. Cascarilla Powder (dried, powdered eggshells)

Controlling Oil

1 1/2 cup Almond or Safflower oil
1/3 cup Cascara Sagrada
1/3 Devil's Shoestring
5 drops Bergamot oil

Pulverize the dried ingredients and combine them with the oil in a jar with a lid. Shake it twice per day for two weeks. Then, strain the liquid. Bottle it and store it in a cool, dark place.

Combine the dried ingredients in a blender or a mortar and pestle and grind them to a fine powder. Place them in a jar with the oil. Tighten down the lid and put it in a warm place for two weeks. Shake it twice per day. Then, strain off the herbs and bottle the liquid.

For extra power, add 5 drops of Bergamot oil.

Courage Oil
For confidence and mental strength

1/4 cup Almond oil
7 drops Geranium
7 drops Rose
7 drops Sweet Pea
7 drops Lavender

Court Case Oil
To win the favor of a judge or jury

1/2 cup Almond oil
10 drops of Galangal (Low John) oil
10 drops of Asafoetida oil
5 drops of Calendula oil
5 drops Snakeroot oil
1 tsp. Slippery Elm powder
1 whole, uncut High John the Conqueror root
Sumac oil (optional)

Add 5 to 10 drops of Sumac oil if you are guilty and in need of leniency. Keep the High John the Conqueror root in the master bottle.

Depending upon how you plan to use it, you may add sugar, syrup or honey to evoke feelings of kindness from the judge, jury or other key players.

Creativity Oil
To promote creativity in the arts and business

1/2 cup Almond oil
2 T. Angelica
1 T. Eyebright
1 T. Rosemary
1 T. Wisteria
Several drops of Sandalwood oil

Combine dried and powdered Angelica, Eyebright, Rosemary and Wisteria into the oil and allow the herbs to macerate for, at least, two weeks. Strain the liquid. Add Sandalwood oil. Store the potion in a dark bottle.

As you prepare this potion, call upon Anatum, Athena, Apollo, Brighid, Danu, Maya, Minerva, Oshun, Odin, Sarasvati, Thoth or the Nine Muses, all of whom are associated with creativity and inspiration, to further empower it.

Dark Arts Oil

1/2 cup Almond oil
Pinch of Valerian root
Pinch of Hairs of a Black Dog
Pinch of Black Mustard seeds
Pinch of Spanish Moss
Pinch of Mullein
Pinch of Sulphur
1/4 tsp. Black Pepper
A rusty nail

Mix and pulverize the dry ingredients, except for the nail. Add them to the Almond oil. Add the nail to the jar and place it in a warm place out of direct sunlight for two weeks. Strain and bottle.

Destroy Enemies Oil

Bone Meal Powder
Palo Muerto (available at online botanicas)
Palo Vence Batalla (available at online botanicas)
Dragon's Blood resin
Twitch Grass

Combine equal parts of the above ground and powdered ingredients into a jar with a tightly fitting lid. Cover this one part mixture of dried herbs with two parts of Almond oil. Allow it to remain in a warm place for, at least, two weeks. Afterward, strain and bottle the oil.

Dixie Love Oil

1/4 cup Almond oil
3 drops Cinnamon oil
5 drops Jasmine oil
7 drops Patchouli oil
Pinch of Bachelor's Button petals

Domination Oil

1/2 cup Almond oil
7 drops Snake oil (Mexican: Aceite de Vibora or Chinese: Enhydris Chinensis)
3 drops Patchouli oil
3 drops Cinnamon oil
3 drops Allspice oil
3 drops Vanilla oil
3 drops Apple Blossom oil

Although the term "snake oil" has come to be a term for quackery in the U.S., in fact, snake oil or powder is a common remedy for joint pain in Mexico. The oil, used topically, is derived from snake meat. In Mexican witchcraft, the snake is a representation of masculine power and domination. Genuine snake oil may be found in Mexican botanicas and online.

There is a similar Chinese remedy made of the Chinese Water Snake, which may be available at some Asian markets.

Double Crossing Oil
Powerful Hoodoo style hexing oil

1 cup Almond oil
2 T. Valerian Root
2 T. Stinging Nettles
2 T. Cayenne Pepper
1 T. Black Pepper
2 T. Patchouli

Combine the above ingredients into a jar with a lid. Place it in a warm spot and shake it twice per day for two weeks. Afterward, strain the liquid into a glass bottle. Store in a cool, dry place out of direct sunlight.

Drive Away Evil

Dragon's blood oil
Garlic oil

Combine equal parts of each. Optionally, add a few drops of Cinnamon oil to expedite the action of the potion.

Eleggua Job Oil
To find a job

1/2 cup of Almond Oil
3 drops Coconut Oil
1 drop Anise Oil
2 drops Orris Oil

Eleggua is the Yoruba Orisha who is the god of crossroads and decision-making. He is syncretically associated with Papa Legba of Haitian Vodou and Saint Anthony in Santeria. He permits or denies communication with the spirits and is appealed to first before contacting any of the others.

Eleggua Money Oil
Use this oil to open the door to money-making

1/2 cup of Almond Oil
7 drops Coconut Oil
1 drop Peppermint Oil
3 drops Sassafras Oil

Eleggua Obstacle Breaker Oil

1/2 cup Almond oil
2 T. Coffee grounds
1 tsp. Saltpeter
3 drops Coconut oil
3 drops Palm oil
Pinch of Sugar
Pinch of dirt from a 4-way crossroad
15 drops Rum

Enmity Oil
To enrage enemies against each other

1 cup Almond oil
9 Pins
9 Needles
9 Rusty Nails
9 Coffin Nails
Hair of Black Cat
Hair of Black Dog
Pinch of Red Pepper
Pinch of Graveyard Dirt

Incantation: "Fight like cats and dogs!"

Erzulie Freda Oil
To attract romance

1/4 cup Almond oil
1 T. Coconut oil
3 Basil leaves
Pinch of Red Rose petals
Vanilla bean

Combine the following ingredients into a bottle. It is not necessary to strain this oil before using it. Optionally, add a drop or two of Basil, Rose or Vanilla oil to strengthen this oil's potency.

Euphoria Oil
To create feelings of happiness and contentment

1/4 cup Hemp oil
1 T. Cat Nip
1 T. Hawthorn
1 T. Passion Flower
1 T. St. John's Wort
1 tsp. Valerian root

Fast Love Oil

1/2 cup Almond oil
3 drops Vanilla oil
10 drops Cinnamon oil
5 drops Lilac oil
5 drops Rose oil

Fast Luck Oil

Citronella oil
Water

Used in potions, including washes to bring money, luck and customers into a place of business. This formula was given by Zora Neale Hurston in *Mules and Men*.[5] The proportions of these ingredients are not specified.

Fiery Wall of Protection Oil
For strong psychic and astral protection

1/2 cup Almond oil
1 T. Dragon's Blood resin
1 T. Frankincense resin
1 T. Myrrh resin
1 T. Ginger, dried and powdered

Combine powdered dry ingredients and oil in a jar. Optionally, add a pinch of sea salt for added potency. Place the jar in a warm place out of direct sunlight for two weeks. Strain and bottle. Store in a cool, dark place.

Flying Devil Oil
For banishing, exorcism and curse reversal

1 cup Almond oil
2 T. Black Seed oil
1 T. Jalepeno seeds
1 T. Red Pepper seeds
1 T. Black Pepper
1 tsp. Mediterannean Oregano oil
1 T. Vetivert

Follow Me Boy Oil No. 1

1/2 cup Almond oil
7 drops Frankincense oil
3 drops Honeysuckle oil
3 drops Vetivert oil
3 drops Vanilla oil

Follow Me Boy Oil No. 2

1 cup Almond oil
1 T. Orris root
1 T. Catnip
1 T. Calamus
1 T. Damiana
1 T. Jasmine
1 T. Licorice

Macerate the dried herbs in oil for, at least, two weeks. Strain and bottle. Optionally, add several drops of Neroli oil.

Follow Me Boy Oil No. 3

1 cup Almond oil
16 drops Calamus root oil
15 drops Catnip oil
15 drops Damiana oil
7 drops Frankincense oil
3 drops Honeysuckle oil
3 drops Vetivert oil
3 drops Vanilla oil

Follow Me Girl Oil

2 cups Almond oil
9 drops Ambrette oil
1/8 cup Birth Root
1/8 cup Calamus root
1/8 cup Cubeb
1/8 cup Damiana
1/8 cup Ginger
1/8 cup Sampson Snake root
1/8 cup High John the Conqueror root
High John the Conqueror or Calamus root
A few hairs from a loyal pet, preferably your own

Combine equal parts of the above herbs and allow them to macerate in oil for, at least, two weeks. Strain the liquid and bottle it. Place a whole root of High John the Conqueror or Calamus in the master bottle and add a few pet hairs.

Funerary Oil
For use at funeral ceremonies

4 parts Camphor oil
4 parts Eucalpytus oil
1 part Tea Tree oil

Get Out of Jail Oil
Use for any situation involving confinement

1/2 cup Almond oil
7 drops Dragons Blood
1 tsp. Coconut oil
7 drops Nutmeg oil

God and Goddess Oil

1/2 cup Almond oil
15 drops Frankincense oil
7 drops Myrrh oil
5 drops Cedar oil

Habondia Oil
To honor the Celtic witch-goddess Habondia, Goddess of Abundance

1/4 cup Grapeseed oil
3 drops Agrimony oil
3 drops Calendula oil
3 drops Chamomile
7 drops Gold of Pleasure (Camelina or False Flax) oil

Has No Hanna Oil
Hoodoo gambling and good luck

1 cup Almond oil
1/4 cup Night Jasmine blossoms

This old Hoodoo formula has been the subject of some controversy. In *Mules and Men*, Zora Neale Hurston indicates that Has No Hanna is Jasmine, however, it appears that it is not the common species, but a Night Blooming Jasmine of the botanical name Cestrum Nocturnum. It is native to the West Indies and South Asia and is commonly called Hasna Hena.

Hex Breaking Oil

1/2 cup Almond oil
3 drops Hyssop oil
3 drops Myrrh oil
3 drops Holy Thistle oil
3 drops Wintergreen oil

Hexing Oil

1/2 cup Almond oil
2 T. Bilberry
1 T. Valerian Root
1 T. Stinging Nettles
1 tsp. Cayenne Pepper
1 tsp. Black Pepper
1 tsp. Tobacco ashes
Pinch of Graveyard Dirt

Pulverize the dry ingredients and combine them with the oil in the jar. Keep it in a warm place away from direct sunlight for two weeks.

High John the Conqueror Oil
To dominate and succeed in love, gambling, financial matters and court cases

3 parts Almond Oil
1 part High John the Conqueror root, powdered

It is difficult to find High John the Conqueror essential oil. Use the above formula to make your own oil infusion. Pulverize the root and place it in a jar with the oil. Keep it in a warm place away from direct sunlight for two weeks. Strain the root out and bottle it. Place a whole root in the master bottle.

Many magical High John the Conqueror formulas purchased from magical suppliers contain other ingredients besides High John. You may follow this example by adding several drops of Dragon's Blood or Myrrh oil to enhance the power of this potion.

Inspiration Oil
To call the muses

3/4 cup Almond oil
2 T. Amber resin
2 T. Angelica
2 T. Cinquefoil
Silver coin

Combine the above herbs in oil. Strain after, at least, two weeks and place a silver coin in the master bottle.

Initiation Oil
For use in coven or self-initiation rites

1/2 cup Almond oil
3 drops Frankincense oil
3 drops Myrrh oil
1 drop Sandalwood oil

Intranquility Oil
To summon the Intranquil Spirit

1 cup Sunflower oil
5 drops Coconut oil
3 drops Lavender oil
2 drops Violet oil or the tops of 2 or 3 blossoms
Pinch of Black Pepper
2 drops Ginseng extract
3 drops of Allspice oil or a pinch Allspice, powdered
Pinch of Knotweed, powdered
Pinch of Stinging Nettles

Invisibility Oil

1/2 cup Almond oil
1 T. Amaranth, dried and powdered
1 T. Chicory dried and crushed
1 T. Edelweiss
1 T. Heliotrope
1 tsp. Poppy seeds
Bloodstone chip

Combine the herbs and pulverize them. In a jar with a tight lid combine the herbs with the oil and shake well. Allow this mixture to stand in a warm place, out of direct sunlight for, at least, two weeks. Strain the liquid. Add a bloodstone chip and the three whiskers to the master bottle.

Isis Oil
For increased mental powers and focused concentration

1/4 cup Almond oil
4 drops Basil oil
4 drops Bay oil
7 drops Calamus oil
7 drops Orris root oil

Jezebel Oil
Do as I say

1/2 cup Almond oil
2 tsp. Calamus
1 tsp. Catnip
2 tsp. Jezebel root
2 tsp. Lavender
2 tsp. Rosemary
2 tsp. Red Rose buds

Jockey Club Oil No. 1
English Formula

1 cup Almond oil
32 drops (2 ml) Orris root oil
16 drops (1 ml) Rose oil
10 drops Cinnamon oil
10 drops Tuberose oil
8 drops Amber oil
4 drops Bergamot oil

This is a classic oil used to obtain work, to command respect, attract good friends and for fast luck and gambling.

This English formula and the French formula below are based on recipes given in Godey's Lady's Book, which was published in the U.S. during the 19th century pre-Civil War Era.[6]

Jockey Club Oil No. 2
French Formula

1 cup Almond oil
16 drops (1 ml) Rose oil
16 drops (1 ml) Tuberose oil
5 drops Cassia oil
5 drops Jasmine oil
3 drops Amber or Ambrette oil

The original formula calls for Civet Cat oil, which is obtained from an endangered species.[7] Amber or Ambrette oil is substituted here.

To make Jockey Club Cologne, omit the Almond oil base. Instead, combine the other ingredients in this potion to a base of 7 parts distilled water and 3 parts Everclear grain alcohol or Vodka.

Add a few drops of Geranium oil to this formula to impart courage, confidence and protection.

Just Judge Oil
For justice and leniency in court

1 cup Almond oil
3 pieces of Galangal root or 8 to 10 drops of Galangal oil
8 to 10 Carnation petals
5 drops Marigold oil or the petals of one or two Marigold blossoms
5 drops Anise oil
5 drops Cinnamon oil
5 drops Rosemary oil

King Midas Touch Oil
To obtain great wealth

1 cup Sunflower oil
7 Basil leaves or 2 T. dried Basil
1/4 cup Calendula
2 T. Chamomile
1 T. Myrrh
A gold ring or gold coin in the master bottle

You may use a different gold object, but it must be whole and unbroken.

Love Attraction Oil No. 1

1/2 cup Almond oil
5 drops Patchouli oil
1 drop Cinnamon oil
1 drop Rosemary oil
1 drop Rose oil

Love Attraction Oil No. 2

1/2 cup Almond oil
3 drops Cypress oil
3 drops Rose oil
3 drops Vanilla oil

Love Attraction Oil No. 3

1/2 cup Almond oil
3 drops Rose oil
3 drops Jasmine oil
3 drops Patchouli oil
7 drops Dragon's Blood oil (made from the resin)
1 small Rose Quartz gemstone
3 red or pink Rose buds

Love Attraction Oil No. 4

1/2 cup Almond oil
3 drops Anise oil
2 drops Cinnamon oil (omit if you have sensitive skin)
3 drops Clove oil
3 drops Sassafras oil

For use by a man, add a whole High John the Conqueror Root to the bottle. Allow this mixture to sit in a warm place out of the direct sun.

Love Attraction Oil No. 5
Based on a formula from the Philippines

1/8 cup Bee's Wax
2 T. Birth Root, powdered
2 T. Deer Antler, powdered
1/8 cup Mineral Oil
1 T. Sea Salt

Warm the bee's wax in a double boiler. Add approximately equal parts of oil. Add Salt, Birth Root and Deer Antler.

Love Binding Oil
To bind lovers together

1/2 cup Almond oil
A few Grape Leaves
A few Verbena leaves
Pinch of Pink Bed Sheets, used, ground and powdered
A few Rose petals
1 tsp. Cinnamon
1 tsp. Clove

Pulverize these ingredients and combine them in the oil for, at least, two weeks. Afterward, strain the liquid and bottle it.
This oil can be combined with other perfumes.

Love Drawing Oil

1/2 cup Almond oil
3 drops Palma Rosa oil
5 drops Ylang-ylang oil
1 drop Ginger oil
3 drops Jasmine oil
2 drops Rosemary oil
5 drops Patchouli oil
3 drops Vanilla oil

Lover Return Oil No. 1

1/2 cup Almond oil
1 T. Calamus root, dried and powdered
1 T. Catnip, dried and powdered
Handful of Daisy petals
1 T. Damiana leaves, dried and powdered
Handful of Red Rose petals or substitute 1 T. powdered, dried Rose Hips

Crush the herbs and allow them to stand in the oil for, at least, two weeks before straining and bottling the liquid.

Lover Return Oil No. 2

1 cup Almond or Safflower oil
7 drops Rose oil or Rose Geranium oil
7 drops Jasmine oil
7 drops Gardenia oil
7 drops Violet oil or 3 or 4 violet blossoms
1 T. Catnip, dried and powdered
Orris Root (optional)

Use the Orris root for potions intended to be used by a woman.

Luck in Court Oil

3 drops Geranium
3 drops Lavender
3 drops Verbena
1 oz. Jockey Club

Two recipes for Jockey Club Oil and one for Jockey Club Powder are given in this book. This formula is derived from information given in Zora Neale Hurston's book *Mules and Men*.

Lucky Dream Oil
*To dream your lucky numbers or the
outcome of an event*

1/2 cup Hemp oil
7 drops Calendula oil
7 drops Frankincense oil
7 drops Heliotrope oil
7 drops Mimosa oil
7 drops Jasmine oil
7 drops Sandalwood oil

Lust and Seduction Oil

1/2 cup Almond oil
3 drops Ambergris oil
3 drops Sandalwood oil
3 drops Frankincense oil
3 drops Patchouli oil
Pinch of Deer's Tongue powder
Orris or High John the Conqueror root

Wear this oil to inspire lust and seduce another person. If the potion is to be used by a woman, add a whole Orris Root to the mixture. If it is to be used by a man, add a whole High John the Conqueror root.

Money Drawing Oil

1/2 cup Almond oil
7 drops Bay oil
7 drops Bayberry oil
7 drops Benzoin oil
7 drops Rue oil
7 drops Sandalwood oil

Ogun Lucky Oil
To honor and petition the Orisha Ogun

1/4 cup of Almond Oil
3 drops Coconut Oil
1 drop Nutmeg Oil
5 drops Strawberry Oil
1 drop Sweet Pea Oil

Ogun Protection Oil

1/4 cup Almond oil
7 drops Rosemary oil
7 drops Eucalyptus oil
Pinch of Sea Salt

Pay Me Oil
To receive payment of a debt owed

1 cup Almond oil
2 T. Calamus
2 T. Lavender
2 T. Orris
2 T. Sage
High John the Conqueror root in the master bottle

Power Drawing Oil
For strength

1/2 cup Almond oil
3 drops Frankincense oil
2 drops Myrrh oil
2 drops Sandalwood oil
1 drop Orange oil
1 drop Lemon oil

Prosperity Oil

1/2 cup Almond oil
3 drops Allspice oil
3 drops Basil oil
3 drops Bayberry oil
3 drops Honeysuckle oil
3 drops Magnolia oil
3 drops Patchouli oil
3 drops Pine oil

Protection Oil
To stop psychic attacks and nightmares

1/2 cup Almond oil
7 drops Basil oil
7 drops Purslane oil
7 drops Sandalwood oil
Lepidolite chip in the master bottle

Psychic Oil

1/4 cup Almond oil
7 drops Frankincense
7 drops Marigold
8 drops Mugwort
7 drops Sandalwood
8 drops Thyme

Rage of Fury Oil
To make enemies fight each other

1/4 cup Almond oil
1 tsp. Black Mustard seeds
1 tsp. Black Pepper
3 drops Capsicum oil
Pinch of Guinea Pepper grains
9 drops Patchouli oil
1 tsp. Red Pepper seeds

Red Carpet Oil
To be treated like a V.I.P.

1 cup Almond oil
2 T. Rose petals
2 T. Marigold blossoms
2 T. Plumeria blossoms
1 T. Iron Weed
Pyrite or Fire Opal in the master bottle

Red Fast Luck Oil
For good luck and to draw customers to your business

Cinnamon oil
Vanilla oil
Wintergreen oil

Combine equal parts of the above. Add a small amount of carrier oil. This potion is based on Red Fast Luck given by Zora Neale Hurston in *Mules and Men*.[8]

Reducing Oil
For weight loss spells

1/4 cup Coconut oil
1 T. Chives
1 T/ Kelp
1 T. Peppermint or 5 drops Peppermint oil
1 T/ Wisteria or 5 drops Wisteria oil

Reverse the Curse Oil
To return hexes to the sender

1/2 cup Almond oil
2 T. Agrimony
1 T. Alum root
2 T. Bilberry Sulfur
2 T. Twitch Grass

Add a pinch of Dragon's blood or Myrrh resin or a few drops of oil to heighten the power of this formula.

Road Opener Oil
To destroy obstacles and pave the way to success in any endeavor

1/2 cup Almond oil
9 drops Citronella oil
3 drops Cinnamon oil
9 drops Cedar oil
9 drops High John the Conqueror Oil
9 drops Palmarosa oil
9 drops Vanilla oil
High John the Conqueror Root in the master bottle

Saint Cyprian Oil
To gain mastery of occult knowledge

1/2 cup Almond oil
1 T. King Solomon's Seal root, powdered
1 T. Heliotrope
1 T. Lilac
1 T. Hyssop
1 T. Rose petals

Powder the dried flower petals and root. Combine them in a jar with the Almond oil. Cover it with a lid and allow it to sit in a warm place out of direct sunlight for two weeks.

Saint Expedite Oil
For expedience

1/4 cup Almond oil
9 drops Allspice oil
9 drops Sandalwood oil
9 drops Honeysuckle oil
3 whole Allspice berries in the master bottle

Saint Jude Oil

1/4 cup Olive oil
2 T. dried Rue or 10 drops Rue oil

Say the following prayer over the oil:

"O Holy St. Jude, glorious apostle, faithful servant and friend of Jesus, pray for me that I may receive the consolations and the succor of heaven in all of my necessities, tribulations and sufferings, particularly [state your desire] and that I may bless God with the Elect throughout Eternity. Amen."

Use this oil to anoint a St. Jude 7-day candle and make your petition. When St. Jude grants your wish, you must place an ad, publicly thanking him.

Saint Lucy Oil
To petition Saint Lucy, patron saint of writers, salesmen and those with visual problems.

1/4 cup Almond oil
7 drops Chamomile
7 drops Eyebright
7 drops Heliotrope

Saint Martha the Dominator Oil
Controlling, commanding, protection, used by women to command a lover

1/4 cup Almond oil
3 drops Dragon's Blood oil
3 drops Hyssop oil
3 drops Spikenard oil
Calamus root in the master bottle

Saint Martin Caballero Oil
For prayers and petitions to Saint Martin Caballero, also, known as Saint Martin of Tours, a powerful ally for the safety, peace and prosperity of your home and business

1/4 cup Almond oil
2 T. Brown Mustard seeds
2 T. Anise seeds
7 drops Cinnamon oil
7 drops Lavender oil

Crush the mustard and anise seeds and put them in a jar with a tightly fitting lid. Then, add the oils. Allow this mixture to remain in a warm place out of direct sunlight for a couple of weeks, after which you may strain the seeds from the potion and place the liquid in a bottle with a lid.

Saint Michael Oil or Archangel Michael Oil
For powerful angelic protection

1/2 cup Almond oil
7 drops Dragon's Blood oil
7 drops Frankincense oil
7 drops Hyssop oil
7 drops Lavender oil
7 drops Myrrh

Saint Simon Oil
To petition San Maximon of Guatemala

1/4 cup Almond oil
3 drops Orange oil
3 drops Lemongrass oil
3 drops Spikenard (or Citronella) oil

Sales Oil
To increase sales

1/4 cup Almond oil
7 drops Bay oil
7 drops Bayberry oil
7 drops Cinnamon oil
7 drops Sandalwood oil

Separation Oil
To break up a couple

1 cup Almond oil
2 T. Chili Powder
1 T. Cinnamon
2 T. Galangal (Low John)
2 T. Black Pepper
2 T. Iron Filings
2 T. Vetivert

Add nettles to this formula to make it sting! Further enhance its power by adding a broken necklace chain.

Seven African Powers Oil No. 1
For protection, luck, money and success

1/2 cup Safflower oil
1/2 cup Cotton Seed oil
1 T. Camphor oil
1 T. Coconut oil
10 drops Palma Christi oil
10 drops Frankincense oil
10 drops Myrrh oil
10 drops Cinnamon oil
10 drops Sage oil
10 drops Sandalwood oil
10 drops Dragon's Blood oil

Seven African Powers Oil No. 2

1 cup Almond oil
1 T. Coconut oil
10 drops Frankincense oil
10 drops Myrrh oil
10 drops Palma Christi oil
10 drops Sage oil
10 drops Sandalwood oil
10 drops Dragon's Blood oil
10 drops Vanilla oil
10 drops Sweet Pea oil
10 drops Allspice oil
5 drops Cinnamon oil

Seven African Powers Oil No. 3

1 cup Safflower oil
7 drops Allspice oil
7 drops Ambrosia oil
1 T. Coconut oil
7 drops Peppermint oil
7 drops Ambergris oil
7 drops Cinnamon oil
7 drops Lemon oil
7 drops Palma Christi oil
7 drops Sandalwood oil
7 drops Vanilla oil

Sexual Power Oil
To attract sexual partners

1/2 cup Almond oil
3 drops Ginger oil
3 drops Patchouli oil
1 drop Cardamom oil
3 drops Sandalwood oil
3 drops Dragon's Blood oil

Success and Domination

1/2 cup Almond oil
1 T. Basil
2 T. Calamus
1 T. Cinquefoil (Five Finger Grass)
4 T. High John the Conqueror Root
1 T. Lemongrass
1 T. Lavender
High John the Conqueror root in the master bottle

Mix and pulverize the dry ingredients and combine them with the oil into a jar. Place the jar in a warm place out of direct sunlight for two weeks. Strain and bottle.

Success in All Endeavors

1/4 cup Almond oil
7 drops Amber oil
7 drops Bay Leaf oil
7 drops Juniper oil
7 drops Lemon Balm oil
7 drops Myrrh

Success in Business Oil

Combine equal parts of the following essential oils in a small amount of carrier oil:

Anise
Bergamot
Cinnamon
Geranium
Lavender
Orange blossom
Rosemary
Wintergreen

Sugar Daddy or Sugar Mama Oil
To attract a generous benefactor

1 cup Almond oil
1 T. Coltsfoot
1 T. Cloves
2 T. Orris root
1 T. Poppy seeds
2 T. Snake Root
2 T. Violet

Super Fast Luck Oil

1 cup Almond oil
1 T. Basil
1 T. Calendula
1 T. Cinnamon
1 T. Patchouli or 5 drops Patchouli oil
1 T. Peppermint or 5 drops Peppermint oil
1 T. Pine Needles
1 T. Vanilla
1 T. Wintergreen or 5 drops Wintergreen oil

Combine powdered, dry ingredients with oil in a lidded jar and set it in a warm place out of direct sunlight for two weeks. Strain through cheesecloth and bottle. Store in a cool, dark place.

Third Eye Opening Oil
To enhance psychic abilities

1/4 cup Almond oil
2 drops Pine oil
1 drop Ginger oil
1 drop Cinnamon oil
1 drop Sandalwood oil

Three Jacks and a King Oil
For gambling and fast luck

1/2 cup Almond oil
5 drops Cinnamon oil
5 drops Carnation oil
5 drops Wisteria oil
5 drops Orange oil

Three Kings Oil
For work with angelic spirits

1/4 cup Almond oil
1 T. Frankincense
1 T. Myrrh
1 T. Citronella

Combine powdered, dry ingredients with oil in a lidded jar and set it in a warm place out of direct sunlight for two weeks. Strain through cheesecloth and bottle. Store in a cool, dark place.

Tranquility Oil
For calm and clear thinking

1/2 cup Almond oil
Bay oil
Basil oil
Flax seed
Lemon Balm
Lavender
Passion flower

Uncrossing Oil No. 1
For uncrossing on a mental, emotional and psychological level

1/2 cup Almond oil
7 drops Bay oil
7 drops Hyssop oil
7 drops Lavender oil
7 drops Rose oil
7 drops Verbena oil
7 drops Vetivert oil (or a root may be added to the bottle)

Uncrossing Oil No. 2
Similar to Uncrossing Oil No. 1

1/2 cup Almond oil
7 drops Citronella oil
7 drops Jasmine oil
7 drops Rose oil
7 drops Violet oil

This is a higher vibratory formula, which is helpful in cases of psychic attack and emotional disturbance. Optionally, add a little Verbena to increase the power of this formula. Angelica, Broom or Lemon may be added to this or other Uncrossing formulas for added purification and protection.

Uncrossing Oil No. 3
For uncrossing on a lower astral, etheric and more densely physical level

1/2 cup Almond oil
7 drops Black Pepper oil
7 drops Cassia oil
7 drops Dragon's Blood oil
7 drops Patchouli oil

Add a pinch of Broom or Angelica root to the bottle for added protection. Add a few drops of Copal to attract helpful spirits. Add several drops each of Bay and Clove oils if the crossing pertains to luck, money or material success.

Van Van Oil No. 1

To clear the way, expedite the action of potions and for good luck

In Hoodoo, Van Van is used to attract good luck and to increase the power of any other spell.

This is a very versatile formula. It is often used as a base or an additional ingredient to other formulas and is helpful in cases where you want to speed the action of another formula or if you feel some obstacle needs to be cleared out of the way.

This formula is based on one described by Catherine Yronwode of Lucky Mojo (www.luckymojo.com).

1/2 cup of Almond oil
16 drops Lemongrass oil
8 drops Citronella oil
1 drop Vetivert oil
1 drop Palmarosa oil
1 drop Ginger Grass oil

You may, also, add a few small pieces of pyrite to the master bottle.

Use Van Van to dress your lodestones and other talisman's. Van Van is protective and helps clear the way for opportunities in your life.

Van Van Oil No. 2

In *Mules and Men* by Zora Neale Hurston, Van Van oil is described as nothing more than Lemongrass oil in alcohol.[9] Proportions are not given. Despite this, some researchers assert that the term "Van Van" is a corruption of Vervain and that this is the main ingredient.

Veritas Oil
To make someone tell the truth

1/4 cup Almond oil
1/8 cup Bluebell blossoms
1/4 cup Primrose blossoms
1/8 cup Wormwood

Wealthy Wife or Wealthy Husband Oil
Use this oil to attract a wealthy spouse

1 cup Almond oil
1 T. Basil
1 T. Camellia
1 T. Dittany of Crete
1 T. Elder bark
1 T. Violet
Lodestones

Women may add Orris root to the mixture, which is, also, used to inspire generosity in others. Men should add High John the Conqueror Root for extra masculine power. The most important ingredients in this formula are Elder bark and Violet.

Wisdom of King Solomon Oil
Enhanced psychic abilities

1/2 cup Almond oil
4 T. Hyssop blossoms
4 T. Rose blossoms
1/8 cup Solomon's Seal root

Wishing Oil

1 cup Sunflower oil
3 T. Ginseng
3 Hazel nuts
3 T. Job's Tears
3 Peach pits
3 T. dried Periwinkle
9 Pomegranate seeds
3 T. Sage dried and powdered
Oil of 1 Vitamin E capsule as a preservative

Crush and macerate the herbs in the sunflower oil. Allow it to stand for, at least, two weeks in a warm place out of direct sunlight. Strain and place in a dark bottle with a tight lid. Store in a cool place.

Youth and Rejuvenation Oil

1 cup Almond oil
2 T. Cat's Claw
2 T. Cowslip
2 T. Myrtle
2 T. White Potato peelings
1 T. Rosemary
1 T. Sage

Elemental Oils

Prepare these oils during their corresponding days and hours to maximize their potency. Use them when you want to apply the characteristics of these elements to a spell.

Air Oil
For quick wit and increased mental powers

1/4 cup Almond oil
5 drops Benzoin
5 drops Lavender
5 drops Sandalwood
3 drops Neroli

Fire Oil
For strength and vitality

1/4 cup Almond oil
3 drops Ginger
2 drops Rosemary
1 drop Clove
1 drop Petigrain

Water Oil
For emotional harmony and romance

1/4 cup Almond oil
3 drops Palmarosa
2 drops Ylang-Ylang
1 drop Jasmine

Earth Oil
For material concerns

1/4 cup Almond oil
4 drops Patchouli
4 drops Cypress

Sabbat Oils

Sabbat oils are most potent when made on their corresponding days. They are, also, used in each of the celebrations on those days.

Beltane or May Day Oil

1/4 cup Almond oil
5 drops Rose oil
2 drops Dragon's Blood oil
3 drops Coriander oil
4 drops Lily of the Valley oil
2 drops Violet oil
2 drops Honeysuckle oil

Litha or Midsummer Oil (Summer Equinox)

1/4 cup Almond oil
3 drops Wisteria oil
4 drops Lavender oil
4 drops Patchouli oil
3 drops Rosemary oil

Lughnassadh Oil

1/4 cup Almond oil
2 drops Basil oil
3 drops Rose oil
2 drops Rosemary oil
3 drops Yarrow oil

Mabon or Autumn Equinox Oil

1/4 cup Almond oil
4 drops Rosemary
4 drops Frankincense oil
2 drops Thyme oil
1 drop Chamomile oil

Halloween or Samhain Oil

1/4 cup Almond oil
3 drops Rosemary oil
3 drops Pine oil
3 drops Bay oil
2 drops Patchouli oil

Yule Oil

1/4 cup Almond oil
2 drops Cinnamon oil
2 drops of Clove oil
2 drops Frankincense oil
2 drops Myrrh oil
1 drop of Orange oil
4 drops of Pine oil

Imbolc (Candlemas) Oil

1/4 cup Almond oil
3 drops Clove oil
2 drops Dragon's blood oil
3 drops Frankincense oil
2 drops Jasmine oil
2 drops Lavender oil
2 drops Rose oil
2 drops Sandalwood oil
3 drops Wisteria oil

Ostara or Spring Equinox Oil

1/4 cup Almond oil
4 drops Lavender oil
2 drops Primrose oil
2 drops Thyme oil

Planetary Oils

Planetary oils are best when created on their corresponding days at the corresponding planetary hours. Use the oils for spells pertaining to the nature of each planet. Each planetary oil calls for a particular gemstone chip to be placed in the bottle.

Sun Oil

1/2 cup Almond oil
10 drops Palma Christi oil
3 drops Sandalwood oil
2 drops Orange oil
2 drops Helichrysum oil
Sunstone chip in the master bottle

Mercury Oil

1/2 cup Almond oil
1 drop Palma Christi oil
3 drops Honeysuckle
3 drops Sweet Pea oil
Lapis Lazuli chip in the master bottle

Venus Oil

1/2 cup Almond oil
10 drops Palma Christi oil
3 drops Amber Gris oil
2 drops Verbena oil
2 drops Lime oil
1 drop Lotus oil
Emerald chip in the master bottle

Earth Oil

1/2 cup Almond oil
20 drops Palma Christi oil
3 drops Sandalwood oil
2 drops Vetivert oil
2 drops Myrrh oil
2 drops Patchouli oil
2 drops Honeysuckle oil
Obsidian chip in the master bottle

Moon Oil

1/2 cup Almond oil
10 drops Camphor oil
5 drops Palma Christi oil
5 drops Wisteria oil
5 drops Myrrh oil
5 drop Lotus oil
Moonstone chip or silver coin in the master bottle

Mars Oil

1/2 cup Almond oil
1 drop Palma Christi oil
5 drops Carnation oil
5 drops Frankincense oil
5 drops Allspice oil
Lodestone or Red Jasper chip in the master bottle

Jupiter Oil

1/2 cup Almond oil
4 drops Bayberry oil
4 Bergamot oil
4 drops Violet oil
4 drops Honeysuckle oil
Citrine or Topaz chip in the master bottle

Moon Oil

1/2 cup of Almond oil
5 drops Jasmine
5 drops Rose
Moonstone chip in the master bottle.

Saturn Oil

1/2 cup Almond oil
3 drops Palma Christi
3 drops Patchouli oil
3 drops Vetivert oil
3 drops Amber Gris oil
3 drops Rue oil
Blue sapphire or amethyst chip in the master bottle

Uranus Oil

1/2 cup Almond oil
10 drops Palma Christi oil
3 drops Narcissus oil
3 drops Verbena
3 drops Amber Gris
Clear quartz crystal chip in the master bottle

Neptune Oil

1/2 cup Almond oil
4 drops Lotus oil
4 drops Lemon oil
4 drops Jasmine oil
4 drops Rose oil
10 drops Amber Gris oil
5 drops Fish oil (optional)
Coral in the master bottle

Pluto Oil

1/2 cup Almond oil
10 drops Palma Christi
5 drops Blue Sonata
Black Onyx or Topaz in the master bottle

Zodiac Oils

Aries Oil
For increased energy and courage

1/4 cup Almond oil
3 drops Pine oil
3 drops Cypress oil
3 drops Geranium oil

Taurus Oil
For stability and resolve

1/4 cup Almond oil
3 drops Rose oil
2 drops Honeysuckle oil
2 drops Primrose oil

Gemini Oil
For creativity and eloquence in communication

1/4 cup Almond oil
3 drops Bayberry oil
2 drops Sandalwood oil
2 drops Marjoram oil

Leo Oil
For increased intuition and harmony in the home

1/4 cup Almond oil
3 drops Rosemary oil
2 drops Rue oil
2 drops Chamomile oil

Virgo Oil
For situations that require analysis, organization and logic

1/4 cup Almond oil
4 drops Myrrh oil
2 drops Violet oil
1 drop Verbena oil

Libra Oil
For fairness and grace

1/4 cup Almond oil
3 drops Amber Gris oil
2 drops Allspice oil

1 drop Citrus oil
2 drops Rose Geranium oil

Scorpio Oil
For regeneration, renewal and sexual energy

1/4 cup Almond oil
3 drops Jasmine oil
3 drops Gardenia oil
1 drop Lemon oil
1 drop Verbena oil

Sagittarius Oil
For tolerance, joy and understanding

1/4 cup Almond oil
4 drops Bayberry oil
1 drop Violet oil
1 drop Carnation oil

Capricorn Oil
*For material and financial concerns
and to break a habit*

1/4 cup Almond oil
2 drops Patchouli oil
2 drops Sandalwood oil
2 drops Wisteria oil

Aquarius Oil
*For fast growth, humanitarianism and
socially-related concerns*

1/4 cup Almond oil
3 drops Jasmine oil
2 drops Comfrey oil
2 drops Pine oil
2 drops Violet oil

Pisces Oil
For mysticism, inspiration and spiritual matters

1/4 cup Almond oil
4 drops Bergamot oil
2 drop Frankincense oil
1 drop Narcissus oil

Sophia diGregorio

7 OLD TRADITIONAL POTIONS

These historic and traditional formulas come from old grimoires and folklore around the world.

Black Salt
For hexing, exorcism, banishing and protection

Sea Salt
Charcoal
Black Pepper
Optionally, the ashes of pertinent herbs

The Black Salt used in Hoodoo spells is made a number of different ways. Fundamentally, it is blackened salt.

Combine equal parts of sea salt, ordinary charcoal and ground Black Pepper. Blend in the ashes of dried herbs according to the purpose of the salt. Thoroughly blend these ingredients in a mortar and pestle until they become a very fine powder.

Sea salt can, also, be combined with powdered black chalk, which is available from craft stores.

Black Salt used in potions should not be confused with the grey or pink volcanic rock salts sold by the same name, which are used in Indian cuisine.

Cascarilla Egg Shell Chalk

Cascarilla chalk is a protective chalk used in African-based magical practices. In this instance, the term, "Cascarilla," refers to the eggshells used to make the chalk and not to the bark of the Cascarilla tree, which is a medicinal plant native to Peru.

A similar eggshell chalk is said to have been used by the Obeah of Jamaica, powerful African sorcerers whose abilities were feared. Eggshells figure heavily into many Obeah charms and Obeah practitioners were known to cast circles for power and protection drawn with a white chalk made of powdered eggshells. Cascarilla chalk is used in Afro-Caribbean traditions as a substitute for Efun, a white chalk from Africa, which is used to draw on the ground and mark the body with symbols.

1 T. Corn Starch
1 T. White Flour
2 to 3 tsp. Cascarilla Powder (formula below)
3 T. Water
Index card
Piece of adhesive tape

Blend the dry ingredients together thoroughly. Then, add water to make a dough of a thick, but not too dry consistency. Add a little more water if it is too dry and a little more cornstarch if it becomes too watery and thin. For a softer chalk, use a proportion of more cornstarch and less flour.

Roll the dough into a ball and dust it with a little flour to prevent sticking. Then roll it into the shape of a cylinder. Roll an index card around it tightly so it keeps its shape. Tape the card in place. Allow the chalk to dry for approximately three days before using it. Alternatively, pour the dough mixture into a small paper cup or the receptacles of an eggshell carton. This method works better for softer chalk.

Caution: Do not use this chalk on wooden surfaces because it may scratch them.

Cascarilla Powder
For protection and purification

Cascarilla Powder is made entirely from powdered white eggshells. It is used alone or as an ingredient in other formulas.

Place eggshells in a cast iron Dutch Oven or place them on a cookie sheet and cover them with aluminum foil so they will not scorch. Bake them for 10 to 15 minutes at 350 degrees.

Allow the eggshells to cool. Then, pulverize them with a mortar and pestle or a grinder until they are reduced to a fine powder. Store this powder in an airtight container in a cool, dark place.

Demon Detector
To alert you to the presence of demonic entities, including vampires, zombies and shape shifters

Acacia bark
Coconut oil (preferably made during Holy Week: From Lazarus Saturday until the day before Easter)
Dragon's Blood
Coral, powdered
Coconut leaves (substitute coconut meat)
A piece of granite
A piece of paper upon which to write a short prayer

The above is based on a formula from the Philippines designed to detect the presence of an Aswang.[10] The Aswang is a shape shifting demonic entity, with the facial characteristics of a dog with bat's wings, although it can take on many other forms. The Aswang is well-known and very much feared, especially in rural areas of the country. It can be traced to, at least, the 16th century in the Philippines with the arrival of the Spaniards.

It is a shape shifter with many of the characteristics of a vampire, zombie or demonic entity. It can be stopped by a silver bullet, a silver sword, garlic, feathers, a broomstick with the bristles hanging upward by the door, a needle stuck in the door or a needle with a broken eye stuck in the threshold.

When this potion begins to boil, a demon is nearby. In the Philippines a sharpened bamboo spear is thrown to destroy the Aswang.[11]

The original formula contains a different species of palm fruit (Bunga ng Niyog) and coconut leaves. If the leaves cannot be easily obtained, substitute coconut flesh. The original formula calls for a piece of granite from the City of Buhay in the Philippines (Batong Buhay). Granite is a combination of crystal and feldspar, which serves as an excellent "battery" for this potion.

To create the demon detecting oil, combine a small amount of each of Acacia bark, Dragon's Blood resin, powdered coral, Coconut leaves or meat and a piece of granite into the oil inside a clear, glass bottle.

Write the following prayer on a plain piece of paper. Recite the prayer, making the sign of the cross over the potion with your forefinger and middle finger at the "+." Then, roll the paper up and place it inside the bottle. Cork the bottle and seal it with wax. Place the bottle near a window where you sleep.

Latin prayer of exorcism:

"Ecce Crucem Domini! +
Fugite partes adversae! +
Vicit Leo de tribu Juda, +
Radix David! Alleluia!"

English Translation:

"Behold the Cross of the Lord! +
Be gone all evil powers! +
The Lion of the tribe of Judah, +
The root of David has conquered! Alleluia!"

Florida Water No. 1

2 drams Sweet Orange oil
6 drams Bergamot oil
6 drams of Lavender oil
2 drops of Neroli oil
20 drops Rose Geranium oil
10 drops Cinnamon oil
10 drops Clove oil
15 drops Sandalwood oil
5 drops Allspice oil
5 drops Lemongrass oil
1 oz. Rose Water (100% Pure - Recipe below)
14 oz. Cologne Spirits (Substitute Everclear grain alcohol or Vodka)

This formula is based on Florida Water from the *Practical Handbook of Toilet Preparations and Their Uses, Also Recipes for the Household*, by Joseph A. Begy.[12] It is true to the original 19th century formula except for the omission of 1 dram (approximately 3/4 tsp.) of chloroform. Chloroform is a sweet-smelling liquid, which has been omitted because it has been determined to be carcinogenic and poisonous. Consequently, like so many old potion ingredient, its modern use is limited.

Combine the above ingredients into a bottle with a tight lid. Shake the contents and let it stand for, at least, four days. It should become cloudy. Then, filter it through a paper coffee filter. Place it in a dark bottle and store it in a cool, dark place.

Rose Water

Rose water is created through a process of distillation in which steam is created by the boiling of the rose petals and collected in a receptacle.

You will need the following:

A stainless steel stock pot with a convex lid
A stainless steel bowl small enough to fit inside the stock pot with, at least, a 1" space around it
A brick
1 to 2 quarts of fresh Rose petals
Distilled Water
Ice cubes

Place the stock pot on the stove. Place the brick inside. Sprinkle the petals all around the brick, but not on top of it. Add enough water to cover the roses, but do not cover the surface of the brick. Place the bowl on top of the brick. Place the lid upside down, so that the curved side is facing downward into the pot.

Allow the pot to come to a boil. Place some ice on top of the concave surface of the lid. This helps to create more steam. Do not allow the pot to boil dry. Your final product should have the sweet smell of roses. Use your Rose Water immediately. Add it to love potions and beauty cremes. Keep any extra Rose Water refrigerated.

Florida Water No. 2

16 oz. of Distilled Water
2 oz. of Vodka
6 drops of Bergamot oil
15 drops Cinnamon oil
3 drops of Clove oil
3 drops of Lavender oil
20 drops Lemon oil

This formula is based on a Florida Water recipe from the book, *Household Cyclopedia of General Information, Containing Over 10,000 Receipts, In All the Useful and Domestic Arts, Constituting a Complete and Practical Library, Relating to Agriculture, Angling, Bees, Bleaching, Keeping, Brewing* by Thomas Kelly, published in 1881.[13]

Flying Ointment - Traditional
This formula is given for purposes of historical information only and is not to be used

Some Western Europeans of a few centuries ago seem to have been very reckless with herbs, particularly some of those of the Nightshade family, such as Datura, Beladonna, European Mandrake and Wolfberry, which are poisonous and may prove deadly if ingested. Such poisons and hallucinogens as these and others were combined with lard or oil to make an ointment.

It is said that these ointments were used by witches to attend Sabbats, during which they cavorted with devils. And, it may be that those who used such flying potions genuinely believed this to be true, although their experiences were, in fact, nothing more than very vivid dreams. There is an account to this effect given by Eusebe Salvarte in *The Occult Sciences: The Philosophy of Magic, Prodigies, and Apparent Miracles*, which describes the following anecdote attributed to a 16th century magistrate of Florence Italy named Paolo Minucci.

A woman was brought before him who claimed to be a sorceress. She bragged to the judge that if he let her go, she would be present at a Sabbat that night if she were permitted her to go home and use her ointment. The judge agreed to this suggestion. "After being rubbed with fetid drugs, the pretended sorceress lay down and immediately fell asleep; she was tied to the bed, while blows, pricking, and scorching failed to break her slumber." With some difficulty, she was roused from this deep slumber the next day, upon which she "detailed the painful sensations which she had really experienced in her sleep, and to which the judge limited her punishment," apparently convinced that she was not an authentic witch.[14]

A common effect of flying potions, including those derived from the excretions of toads and beetles, involves a sense of flying upon wings and going to another location in a dream state. Those who experienced such dreams were convinced of their reality. Potions similar to these were implicated in cases of insanity.

Grimoires from the Middle Ages give different ingredients for Flying Ointment, which is sometimes called Green Ointment because of its color. The following are ingredients found in traditional recipes, however, they are rarely used and are presented here for informational purposes only because most of these ingredients are deadly poisonous or dangerous hallucinogenics. (Please, see the safer formula below.)

European or English Mandrake
Belladonna
Poplar leaves
Soot
Clove oil
Annamthol
Betel
Cinquefoil
Extract of Opium Poppy
Henbane

Flying Ointment - Modern
Safer

This modern flying ointment is more often used by modern witches because it is considered to be safer, however, it should never be ingested. It should only be applied topically and never consumed.

1/4 cup Lard
1/2 tsp. Clove oil
1 tsp. Chimney Soot
1/4 tsp. Cinquefoil, dried and powdered
1/4 ttsp. Thistle, dried and powdered
1/4 dried Vervain, dried and powdered
1/2 tsp. Benzoin tincture

Melt the lard using low heat. Add all of the remaining ingredients except Clove oil and Benzoin tincture. Stir the mixture in a counter clockwise direction on a low setting for 10 to 15 minutes. Then, remove it from the heat and allow it to cool. Strain the mixture into a jar with a lid.

Add the Clove oil and Benzoin tincture and stir well. Store it in a cool, dark place.

Four Thieves Vinegar

Vinegar
Lavender
Rosemary
Sage
Thyme
Melissa (Lemon Balm)
Hyssop
Peppermint
Crushed Garlic cloves

Pour enough white or apple cider vinegar into the jar to soak the herbs, then pour in more so that the herbs sit in about the lower 1/3 of the jar and the other 2/3 of the volume of the jar is vinegar. Put a lid on it and store it in a warm place out of the direct rays of the sun. Shake it twice per day for two to six weeks. Then, strain the liquid through a piece of cheesecloth or gauze and bottle your Four Thieves Vinegar.

Hex Bane

Hoodoo formula to drive away bad people and bad spirits and to break hexes and curses

Pint Red Wine
1/4 cup Bay leaves
1/4 Blue Vervain
1/8 cup Cinnamon
1/4 cup Hyssop
1/4 cup Sea Salt

Allow the herbs and salt to steep in the wine for, at least, two weeks before straining the liquid and bottling it.

Hoodoo Harming or Killing Potion

Vinegar
Beef Gall
Gumbo File' (ground Sassafras leaves)
Red Pepper

This formula and instructions were given by Zora Neale Hurston in *Mules and Men*. The proportions of these ingredients are not specified.[15]

Beef gall is used for medical purposes. It is the bile of a cow evaporated over a low heat. Gumbo File' is a seasoning used in dishes in the Gulf Coast area of the U.S. It is available in grocery stores; Zatarain is a popular brand. It can be made by pulverizing dried Sassafras leaves.

Place the above ingredients in a bottle with a secure lid. On a small, clean piece of paper, write the victim's name nine times. Turn the paper 90 degrees and write a three to four word phrase over the top of what you have previously written that represents your wish for the victim. Add the paper to the bottle and secure the lid.

Shake the bottle for nine mornings in a row while telling it what you want it to do. To harm or kill the victim, turn it upside down and bury it breast deep and he will die.

Joe Fraser's Hoodoo Hexing Formula

2 eggs
1 pint Kerosene
1 pint Turpentine
Vinegar
1 T. Cayenne Pepper
1 box Salt

The above formula is said to have belonged to a Georgia root doctor named Joe Fraser, who passed his potion book on to a man interviewed by The Georgia Writer's Project and recorded in the book *Drums and Shadows*.[16]

Love Potion No. 9

Serve this love philter to your lover to intensify your relationship. The origins of this spell are uncertain, but it appears to be very old. It contains wine and nine powerful love herbs. This is the only potion in this formulary which may be consumed. Therefore, it should be used as is without making any substitutions for ingredients.

Begin brewing this potion on September 9th at the 9th hour of the day.

As you make Love Potion No. 9, consider all of the ways you can incorporate the number "9" into its manufacture. Before you begin, light nine pink candles.

Then, combine the following in a pot on the stove:

9 cups sweet Red Wine (or Concord Grape juice)
9 Cinnamon sticks
9 Red Rose petals
9 whole Cloves
9 Apple seeds
9 Anise stars
9 drops Vanilla extract
9 pieces of Ginseng root
Juice from 9 Persimmons

Stir the potion nine times. Each time you stir it pronounce the following incantation:

"When [Name] drinks this wine
He/She will shower me love divine
Potent Love Potion No. 9
Make him/her forever mine."

Bring the potion to a boil, then reduce the heat and allow it to simmer for nine minutes. Then, remove it from the heat.

Blow on the potion nine times while reciting the names of the following nine goddesses of love each time: Inanna, Ishtar, Astarte, Hathor, Nephthys, Aphrodite, Venus, Freya, Arianrhod.

Strain the liquid. Refrigerate it. Do not tell anyone. Don't let anyone else see it or touch it. Serve it to your intended lover within a day or two but do not tell him or her that it is a love potion, lest the effects be lessened or negated.

Move Away
To make a neighbor move

1 pint Urine
3 T. Sea Salt or Black Salt
3 T. Garlic, crushed or oil
1 tsp. Black Pepper

Urine is used in spells to gain control of someone. Traditionally, this formula was tossed onto the property of the enemy. It can, also, be incorporated into spells with candles, images and poppets to represent the enemy. It is similar to War Water, below.

Simple Fluid Condenser
For all occult operations, including both practical and ceremonial magic

This is simple version of a Fluid Condenser adapted from the brilliant Czech occultist Franz Bardon's book, *Initiation into Hermetics*. A similar formula was used by the influential English witch Sybil Leek. It is used to condense the etheric field for manifestation in operations involving summoning.

It sustains the vibrational imprint placed upon it by the sorcerer.

A handful of Chamomile flowers (you may substitute Lily blossoms, Arnica or Aacia)
1 to 2 quarts of distilled water
10 drops Gold Tincture
Vodka, Everclear or other grain alcohol

Begin with a quart of water and a handful of Chamomile flowers. Bring them to a boil, then lower the heat to a high simmer for 20 minutes, watching very carefully to make sure that the liquid doesn't evaporate and scorch the pot. Add water as necessary. Reduce the liquid to approximately 1/4 cup or 50 ml.

Allow it to cool. Then, strain it and place it in a glass bottle. Add an equal volume of Everclear grain alcohol or Vodka to it. Then, add 10 drops of Gold Tincture along with a drop of blood or sperm. Blood or sperm may, also, function as a substitute for Gold Tincture.

Keep the lid tightly on the bottle and shake the potion well before using it. Stored in a dark, cool place, it does not lose its efficacy.

Gold Tincture

Using a pair of tongs, hold a gold coin or ring of, at least, 14k gold over an open flame until it becomes extremely hot. Then drop it into a pot of distilled water of a volume that is approximately 8 times the weight of the gold item and allow it to cool. Repeat this procedure 7 to 10 times.

Universal Fluid Condenser

A more powerful condenser used for materialization and in the creation of familiars and servitors

The procedure for Universal Condenser is similar to the Simple Fluid Condenser, with the exception that instead of Chamomile flowers or a lone substitute a combination of ingredients is used to make the decoction. The steps thereafter, including the addition of the Gold Tincture, are identical.

Combine equal amounts of the following:

Angelica root
Chamomile
Cinnamon
Cucumber skin
Lime tree blossoms
Melon seeds
Sage
Tobacco leaves, green or dried
Violet blossoms or leaves
Willow bark or leaves

This formula is used in a wide variety of spells to influence the physical, etheric, mental and astral planes by holding and condensing the power placed into it by the practitioner. An in depth description of its uses and variations on the formula for different purposes may be found in *Initiation Into Hermetics: A Course of Instruction of Magic Theory & Practice* by Franz Bardon, wherein the formation of "elementaries," which are similar to the familiars of Western witchcraft, is discussed at length.[17]

Tar Trap Oil
To create a sticky situation for someone

Aloes
Molasses
Turpentine
Creosote, tar balls or other sticky tar-like substance
(Caution: Creosote and tar balls are carcinogenic)
Spanish Moss (optional)
Sulfur (optional)
Gun Powder (optional)

The basis for the idea of creating a device made of tar, resin and other sticky substances in the shape of an animal or human to entrap or bewitch an enemy is ancient and appears to have its origins among the Indians of North America, although similar old tales are told in the Caribbean and throughout Central and South America.

One of the best known of these is the Cherokee folk tale of the rabbit and the tar wolf. A rabbit was suspected of stealing water from a well, so the other animals devised a ball of tar in the form of a wolf to frighten her off. The rabbit was deceived by the tar wolf and believing herself to be insulted by the animal's silence kicked it. The rabbit was then trapped in a sticky mess, which only worsened as she struggled against it.[18]

In magical practice, the sticky substance is formed and placed into a poppet or "voodoo doll." Its purpose is to entrap an enemy in a sticky situation that is worsened by struggling and which is the result of his or her own folly.

Any resinous, tar-like substances will work for this formula. Incorporating personal effects of the victim as well as herbs and other ingredients serve to direct and enhance the purpose of the formula.

War Water

A gallon of Water
Approximately 1/4 pound of real iron nails or iron filings
8 oz. Turpentine (optional)

Add the nails or iron filings to a quart-sized jar and fill the rest of the jar with water. Add the optional turpentine or similar ingredients. Allow this to sit for a couple of weeks until the nails begin to rust and disseminate their particles into the water. Use it to drive away an enemy by pouring it on a place where they must walk.

Some old formulas call for creosote or turpentine, which are derived from pine tar. This variation is sometimes called "Tar Water." Similar sticky substances may be added to this formula to give it extra binding power.

Water Notre Dame
To make peace in the home

White Rose oil
Water

This original potion was given by Zora Neale Hurston in her book, *Mules and Men*.[19] The proportions of White Rose oil to water are not specified. Sprinkle it inside the home.

Witch's Bottle
For counter-magic; to send back black magic

This formula and procedure will have the greatest effect when conducted during the time of Moon in Scorpio.

You will need the following:

A bottle with a tightly fitting cork
Black candle wax, softened
Urine
Hair
Nail Clippings
Bent Needles
Iron Nails
Straight Pins
Knotted thread, ribbon or yarn (preferably black)
Fish Hooks

This formula is based on Witch's Bottles found throughout England and New England. The original bottles were brown Bellarmine jugs imported to England and New England from the Rhineland region of Germany. They were bulbous at the bottom with a narrow neck (similar to the shape of a light bulb), which featured a human face on the side of the bottle.

To make the above formula, use the urine, hair and nail clippings of the bewitched. Add several bent needles, iron nails, straight pins, fish hooks, as well as thorns and any other sharp, treacherous objects. Add wads of knotted up black thread or yarn. The purpose of these items is to entrap the dark energies cast at the victim.

Boil the urine and the above items together. This brings the essence of the spell caster to the surface. Allow the liquid to cool. Pour the liquid and all of the effects into a bottle.

Optionally, you may add a written prayer or petition with protective names or symbols to enhance the effects of this potion. State your purpose, as follows, "Entrap herein all evil and send it back from whence it came." Cork it. Seal the hole with black wax. Also, you may fashion an image on the side of the bottle. This may be constructed of clay or simply a face drawn on paper and affixed to the side of the bottle with tape or glue.

Then, bury the bottle upside down beneath your hearth, near your threshold, under your house or near the foundation. If this is not possible, hide the bottle in the attic, in the basement or in the back of a closet where it won't be found or touched by anyone.

Sophia diGregorio

8 POWDERS

These formulas call for you to pulverize the ingredients. This can be done with an inexpensive coffee grinder, a blender or a mortar and pestle.

Many of the attractive stone and ceramic mortars and pestles sold in metaphysical stores are not sturdy or rough enough to grind some of these ingredients. For heavier use, look for the rougher mortars and pestles, which are often found at Indian (Asian) and Mexican Markets.

Some formulas call for corn starch. At your discretion, you may add a little corn starch to other powder formulas to make them go farther and smooth the texture.

Use herbs in their dried form.

Algiers Powder
For love and luck in gambling

Combine and pulverize equal parts of the following:

Cinnamon
Orris root
Patchouli
Vanilla bean powder

Grind the above ingredients very finely to make this classic powder. Thin it with a little corn starch, if you like. Rub this powder into your palms and rub them together before gambling. Dust your entire body with it before looking for love.

Altar Powder
Sprinkle on your altar to attract spirits

2 T. Jasmine
2 T. Violet
1 tsp. Lavender
1 tsp. Spearmint or Wintergreen leaves

Aphrodisiac Powder

Combine and pulverize equal parts of the following:

Bergamot
Cinnamon
Clove
Ginseng
Tamarind

Astral Travel Powder

Sprinkle this powder on sheets or under pillow before retiring:

1 tsp. Sandalwood
1 tsp. Dittany of Crete
1 tsp. Mugwort
1/4 tsp. Lavender

Attract Good Spirits Powder
To heal and to attract helpful spirits

1 tsp. Orris root
1/2 tsp. Marshmallow root
1/2 tsp. Holly leaves
1/2 tsp. Vanilla bean
1/2 tsp. Clove
Pinch of Lavender herb

Banishing Powder No. 1
To get rid of an enemy

Combine and pulverize equal parts of the following:

Angelica root
Black Pepper
Cayenne Pepper
Clove
Garlic
Graveyard Dirt (preferably gathered at the time of a waning moon on a Saturday night)
Nettles
Sea salt

Banishing Powder No. 1

Combine and pulverize equal parts of the following:

Black Peppercorns
Cayenne
Cinnamon
Sea Salt
Sulphur

Bend Over Powder
Curse reversal, hex breaking and commanding

Combine and pulverize equal amounts of the following:

Allspice
Bergamot
Calamus root
Cinnamon
Frankincense
Honeysuckle blossoms
Licorice root
Vetivert
White Rose petals

Black Devil or You Are Mine Powder
To keep a lover true

Combine and pulverize equal parts of the following:

Bay leaf
Catnip
Cumin
Plumeria
Rosemary
Unicorn Root

Mix with sugar or salt to stop a lover from straying.

Blessing Powder

1 tsp. Angelica
1 tsp. Dragon's Blood resin
3 T. Lavender
1 tsp. Myrrh resin
1/2 tsp. Sea Salt
Pinch of Magnetic Sand (preferably silver)

Boss Fix Powder
To tame a tyrannical employer

2 T. Chili Powder
1 T. Frankincense
2 T. Tobacco ashes
1 tsp. Powdered Newsprint (can be carefully bake dried beneath a glass cake pan)

Pulverize the above ingredients very finely. This powder is often sprinkled around the office of a bullying boss and used in spells to effect change at a distance.)

Clairvoyant Powder
For psychic enhancement

2 T. Mugwort
1 T. Yarrow
1 T. Eyebright
1 T. Lemongrass

Confusion Powder No. 1
Throw your enemy off the track

1 T. Coconut, dried and powdered
1/4 tsp. Black Pepper
1/4 tsp. Ginseng
1/2 tsp. Rue
1/2 tsp. Blueberries, dried and powdered

Confusion Powder No. 2
To leave your enemy bewildered and unable to find you

Combine and pulverize equal parts of the following:

Dirt from a crossroad
Black Pepper
Celandine
Coconut
Devil's Shoestring
Ginseng
Lavender
Violet

Courage Powder
For courage and calm resolution in any situation

Combine and pulverize equal parts of the following:

Amber
Bell Heather
Borage
Rose
Lavender
Lilac

Court Case Powder
To win the favor of a judge or jury

2 tsp. High John the Conqueror
2 tsp. Deer's Tongue
2 tsp. Galangal (Low John)
2 tsp. Snake Root
1 tsp. Cascara Sagrada
1 tsp. Celandine
1 tsp. Hydrangea leaf
1/8 tsp. Asafoetida powder

Crossing Powder
Hoodoo style hexing formula

1 T. Graveyard Dirt (Gathered at midnight from the grave of murder)
1 T. Guinea Pepper
2 T. Pepperwort
2 T. Pine Needles
1 T. Seashells, powdered
4 T. Wormwood

Combine and powder the above dried ingredients. Optionally, add a little powdered Ground Ivy to bind the formula.

Damnation Powder
To curse an enemy

2 T. Boneset
2 T. Cinquefoil (Five Finger Grass)
1 T. Burnt ashes from palm leaves (If possible, Palm leaves from a Catholic Church on Palm Sunday)
1/4 tsp. Lavender
1/2 tsp. Myrrh

Sprinkle a few drops of Holy Water and strong, dark beer into the mixture.

Discover a Thief Powder

Combine equal parts of the following:

Devil's Claw
Galangal
Hydrangea
Poke root
Vetivert

Grind these herbs to a fine powder and sprinkle them around the crime scene to discover the identity of the thief.

Dispel Anger and Hatred

1 tsp. Ashes from incense burned at the dark of the moon with the intention of destroying enmity
1/2 tsp. Jasmine
1/8 tsp. Red Pepper
1/2 tsp. Sandalwood
1/2 tsp. White Rose petal

Dispel Envy and Jealousy

1/2 tsp. Anise
1/2 tsp. Bayberry
1/2 tsp. Vetivert
Pinch of Sassafras
Pinch of Arrowroot powder

Domination Powder

Combine and pulverize equal parts of the following:

Bergamot
Calamus
Licorice Root

Drawing Powder
Attract good spirits and good luck

Combine and pulverize equal parts of the following:

Jasmine
Lavender
Violet

Dream Powder
For prophetic dreams

2 parts Basil
2 parts Mugwort
2 parts Lavender
1 part Silver Magnetic Sand

Dysphoria Powder
To cause worry, anxiety and discomfort

Combine and pulverize equal parts of the following:

Coffee grounds
Ginseng
Guinea Peppers
Iron filings

Euphoria Powder
To create feelings of happiness and contentment

Combine and pulverize equal parts of the following:

Cat Nip
Hawthorn
Passion Flower
St. John's Wort

Exorcism Powder

Combine the following dried and powdered resin and herbs and grind into a fine powder in a mortar and pestle.

4 tsp. Basil
1 tsp. Blessed Thistle
1 tsp. Frankincense
1 tsp. Rosemary
1 tsp. Yarrow Root powder
1/8 tsp. Rue
1/8 tsp. Myrrh

Faithful Lover Powder
To keep a lover from straying

Combine and pulverize equal parts of the following:

Aspen bark or leaves
Chaste Tree berries
Unicorn Root

Fast Love Powder

1/4 cup Corn Starch
3 T. Cinnamon
2 T. Roses
A few Lilac petals
1 tsp. Sugar

Fast Luck Powder

2 T. Gum Mastic
1 tsp. Cloves
1 tsp. Ginger
1 tsp. Lemon Peel
1 tsp. Orange Peel

Fertility Powder
For women who desire greater fertility

Cinnamon
Patchouli
Myrtle
Sage
Vetivert

The most propitious time to make this formula is when the Moon is in Cancer. Sprinkle this powder on your bed, use it in fertility spells and meditations and dust your body with it.

Fidelity Powder No. 1

Combine and pulverize equal parts of the following:

Lime peel
Orange peel
Magnolia
Orris Root
Rosemary
Skullcap

Fidelity Powder No. 2

1 tsp. Allspice
3 tsp. Clove
1 tsp. Deer's tongue
1/2 tsp. Mullein
1/2 tsp. White Sage
Pinch of white bed sheet (Used, burned and pulverized)

Follow Me Boy Powder
To attract and dominate a man

Combine and pulverize equal parts of the following:

Calamus root
Catnip
Damiana
Frankincense
Vetivert

Follow Me Girl Powder
To attract and dominate a woman

Ambrette oil
Birth Root
Calamus root
Cubeb
Damiana
Ginger
Sampson Snake root
High John the Conqueror root

Combine equal parts of dried powdered Birth Root, Calamus, Cubeb, Damiana, Ginger, Sampson Snake, and High John the Conqueror. Mix and pulverize these ingredients. Add several drops of Ambrette oil and mix it thoroughly into the powder.

Forgive and Forget Powder
*To cause someone to forget a wrong or
a debt you owe them*

Combine and pulverize equal parts of the following:

Datura
Poppy seeds
Roses
Rue

Gambling Powder No. 1

1 tsp. Arrowroot
1 tsp. Cinnamon
2 tsp. Cinquefoil (Five Finger Grass)
1 tsp. Comfrey
1/2 tsp. Myrrh
1 tsp. Thyme

Gambling Powder No. 2

2 tsp. Allspice
1 tsp. Heather
2 tsp. High John the Conqueror
1 tsp. Patchouli
1 tsp. Pine Resin

Generosity Powder

Combine and pulverize equal amounts of the following:

Lavender
Orris
Sage

Get a Job Powder
Imparts luck, domination and courage to job seekers

Combine and pulverize equal parts of the following:

Black Pepper
Clove
Ginger
Gravel Root
Lavender
Rose
Ylang-Ylang

Get a Raise Powder

Combine and pulverize equal parts of the following:

Allspice
Bayberry
Bay Leaves
Dragon's Blood
Gravel Root

Glamour Powder
To appear more desirable

Combine and pulverize equal parts of the following:

Anise
Cloves
Rose Hips
Rosemary

Good Business Powder

1 tsp. Frankincense
2 tsp. Irish Moss
2 tsp. Vetivert
1 tsp. Gold or Silver Magnetic Sand

Good Luck Powder No. 1

Combine and pulverize equal parts of the following:

Jasmine petals
Myrrh resin

Good Luck Powder No. 2

1/4 cup Lavender herb
1/4 cup Catnip herb
2 tsp. Marjoram
2 tsp. Cinquefoil (Five Finger Grass)

Goofer Dust No. 1

Combine and pulverize equal parts of the following:

Graveyard Dirt (preferably taken from the grave of a murderer at midnight)
Cayenne Pepper
Sulfur
Ashes from a fire
Powdered bones (Bone Meal)
Iron filings

Add the following:

Pinch of salt
Rattlesnake Skin or Rattle, powdered

The ingredients in Goofer Dust are things designed to poison and kill the victim by means of magic. When it is blessed and carried in a bag with you, it becomes a protective agent.

Powdered rattle snake skin or rattle is a powerful ingredient included in some authentic Goofer Dust formulas.

Goofer Dust No. 2

Graveyard Dirt alone may be used as Goofer Dust. According to Zora Neale Hurston in *Mules and Men*, Goofer Dust includes only this one ingredient.[20] But, many potion-makers like to add increased power and direction to Goofer Dust by including additional ingredients.

In traditional Hoodoo practice, the spirits of the graveyard must be treated with respect. People sometimes pay a few coins at the entryway to a cemetery and request permission from the spirits to enter. If dirt is collected from a grave, it is done with the spirit's permission and a coin is left to pay the spirit. Graveyard Dirt collected for Goofer Dust should be collected during the Dark of the Moon, preferably at midnight. If this is not possible, then go in the day time during an appropriate moon phase.

Habit Breaking Powder
To stop a habit or addictive behavior

Combine and pulverize equal parts of the following:

Patchouli
Sandalwood resin
Wisteria

Healing Powder

1/4 tsp. Allspice
2 tsp. Eucalyptus
1/2 tsp. Myrrh
1/2 tsp. Thyme

Hex Breaking Powder

Combine and pulverize equal parts of the following:

Chili powder
Datura (Caution: Toxic)
Hyssop
Myrrh

High John the Conqueror Powder
For prosperity and to gain dominance over people and situations

Mix and pulverize equal parts of the following:

High John the Conqueror Root
Cinquefoil (Five Finger Grass)
Lavender
Lemongrass

Higher Self Powder
To facilitate communication with guardian spirits

1/4 tsp. Clove powder
1/2 tsp. Hyacinth
1/2 tsp. Lily
1/2 tsp. Pine needles

Hot Foot Powder

Hot Foot Powder is a classic formula for getting rid of unwanted attention, people or energies. Sprinkle it where the person lives, works or must walk. Or, use it in spells by applying it to objects that represent the person, place or idea you want to influence.

1 cup Graveyard Dirt
1 tsp. Sea Salt
1 tsp. Black Pepper
1 tsp. Cayenne Pepper
1 tsp. Red Chili Pepper
1 tsp. Sulfur
1 tsp. High John the Conquer Root, powdered

Increase Power Powder
To add more strength to your spells

Combine and pulverize equal parts of the following:

Almonds
Cascara Sagrada
Cinnamon
Coconut
Myrrh
Sea Salt
Vanilla beans

For even more power, add several drops of Van Van Oil (See recipe under Oils) to the powdered mixture.

Invisibility Powder
*For going into situations in which
you don't want to be noticed*

At the dark of the moon, combine and pulverize equal parts of the following:

Amaranth
Chicory
Edelweiss
Fern leaf
Poppy blossoms and seeds

Isis Powder
Increase your ability to focus and concentrate

1/4 cup Calamus root
1/4 cup Orris root
Pinch of Chamomile
Pinch of Skullcap

Jalop Powder
Strong protection

Combine and pulverize equal parts of the following:

Calamus root
High John the Conqueror root
Low John (Galangal) root
Orris root
Rosemary

Jinx Removing Powder

Combine and pulverize equal parts of the following:

Low John (Galangal) root
Mint leaf
Nettles
Verbena

Job Hunting Powder
For success in getting the next contract, gig or employment situation

Combine and pulverize equal parts of the following:

Gravel Root
Mistletoe
Sea Salt
Woodruff
Yellow Evening Primrose

Jockey Club Powder
Original Formula
To get work, to make people like you, for horse betting, gambling and fast luck

2 oz. Orris root
1/2 tsp. Vanilla beans
1/2 oz. Lavender flowers
2 1/4 tsp. Gum Benzoin
1/2 oz. Orange blossoms
1/2 oz. pale Rose petals
10 grains True Musk Grain (substitute Musk Seed oil)
1 tsp. Sandalwood Oil
10 drops Neroli oil
25 drops Bergamot oil
20 drops Civet oil (substitute Amber oil)

This formula is based on Jockey Club Sachet Powder

from the book, P*ractical Handbook of Toilet Preparations and Their Uses, Also Recipes for the Household*, by Joseph A. Begy.[21]

True Musk Grains are obtained from the gland of a Musk Deer. These are still used in some perfumes and Traditional Chinese Medicine. Civet is derived from the gland of an African cat by the same name. It is a female sex oil, which is said to make any woman irresistible to men. These have become difficult to obtain because of the endangerment of species and greater awareness of cruelty to animals. Therefore, synthetics are used by some perfumers. Amber and Ambrette (Musk Seed) oil are common substitutes for musks and may be used in this formula as substitutes for True Musk and Civet.

Combine the dried ingredients, pulverize and mix. Then combine the oils and blend them together. Add the oil to the powder.

Just Judge Powder No. 1
For success in court cases and to win the favor of a judge

Combine and pulverize equal parts of the following:

Anise seed
Carnation petals
Cinnamon
Low John (Galangal) root
Marigold petals
Rosemary

Just Judge Powder No. 2

1 part Hyacinth
2 parts Patchouli
2 parts Sandalwood
Pinch of Myrrh
Pinch of Low John (Galangal)

Keep Away Powder No. 1

2 T. Sulfur
2 T. Chili Powder
Pinch of Asafoetida

Keep Away Powder No. 2

1 tsp. Red Pepper powder
1/2 tsp. Black Pepper powder
1/2 tsp. Ginger root
1/2 tsp. High John The Conqueror
1/2 tsp. Patchouli

Keep Away Powder No. 3

Combine and pulverize equal parts of the following:

Dirt from a nearby crossroad
Mistletoe
Orris root
Sage
Sulfur

Store in a black bottle or jar until you are ready to use it.

Lion Heart Powder
For the courage of a lion

Combine and pulverize equal parts of the following:

Dragon's Blood
Low John (Galangal) root
Masterwort
Rose
Vanilla

Love and Caring Powder

1 tsp. Gardenia
1 tsp. Lilac
1 tsp. Lily of the Valley
1 tsp. Lily

Love Powder No. 1
To attract love

1 tsp. Cinnamon powder
1 tsp. Orris root
1 tsp. Rosemary
1/2 tsp. Ginger powder
1/2 tsp. Yarrow powder
Several Rose petals

Love Powder No. 2
For love and meditation

3/4 tsp. Benzoic Acid (or Benzoin oil)
1/2 oz. Lily of the Valley
1 1/2 tsp. Mace
3 oz. Orris root
1/2 oz. Peony
1/2 oz. Red Rose leaves
1/2 oz. Violet
5 drops Almond oil
10 drops Cinnamon oil

This formula is based on an old 19th Century Lavender Powder by Joseph A. Begy.[22] Combine dried powdered, dried ingredients first and mix them well. Blend the oils separately. Add the blended oils to the powdered mixture.

Love Powder No. 3
To attract a man

1 part Bachelor's Buttons
1 part Clary Sage
1 part Lavender
Pinch of Sassafras leaf
Pinch of Valerian

Lover's Delight Powder
To release inhibitions

Combine and pulverize equal parts of the following:

Sandalwood resin
Red Rose petals
Quina Roja
Saw Palmetto

Love and Lust Powder

Combine and pulverize equal parts of the following:

Apple Blossom
Lavender
Roses
Violet
Yarrow

Lust Powder

Deer's Tongue
Low John (Galangal) root
Patchouli
Periwinkle

Lucky Gambling Powder

1/2 tsp. Cinnamon
2 tsp. Patchouli
1 tsp. Spearmint leaves

For fast luck, apply this powder to your hands right before gambling.

Money Drawing Powder No. 1

Combine and pulverize equal parts of the following:

Bayberry
Eucalyptus
Marjoram
Pine
Sandalwood
Spearmint

Money Drawing Powder No. 2

1/4 tsp. Cinnamon
1 T. Cinquefoil (Five Finger Grass)
1/4 tsp. Frankincense resin
1/4 tsp. Myrrh resin
1/4 tsp. Patchouli
1 tsp. Sandalwood resin
1 tsp. Yellowdock

Prophetic Dream Powder
For a sachet to be placed under a pillow or used in spells

Combine and pulverize equal parts of the following:

Angelica
Calendula
Jasmine
Lavender
Mugwort
Orris

Prosperity Powder

Combine and pulverize equal parts of the following:

Honeysuckle
Magnolia
Patchouli
Pine

Protection from Evil Powder

2 T. Dragon's Blood (obtain resin in crushed/powdered form)
2 T. Sandalwood
1 T. Myrrh
1 T. Orris Root powder
Pinch of Sea Salt or Black Salt

Psychic Powder
To increase psychic abilities and induce prophetic dreams

1/4 cup Orris Root powder
1 tsp. Amber resin
1 tsp. Chicory
1 tsp. Mugwort
2 tsp. Vetivert

Sprinkle this powder on bed sheets, tarot cards and rune stones or dust some on yourself.

Quitting Powder No. 1
To make married men or women leave you alone

1 T. Almonds (crushed)
1 tsp. Cinnamon
1 tsp. Nutmeg
1 tsp. Tobacco ashes
1 tsp. Newsprint, baked dry beneath a glass cake pan and dried
Pinch of Ashes of Hair from your hair brush, which you have burned

Quitting Powder No. 2
To get rid of nuisance persons

Combine and pulverize equal parts of the following:

Black Pepper
Chili Powder
Ginger
High John The Conqueror
Patchouli
Red Pepper

Red Hot Fast Luck Powder

Combine and pulverize equal parts of the following:

Carnation
Cinnamon
Orange
Vanilla
Wisteria

Repel Evil and Black Magic

Combine and pulverize equal parts of the following:

Eyebright
Mallow
Prunella
St. John's Wort
Speedwell
Vervain
Yarrow

Reverse Bad Luck Powder No. 1

Combine and pulverize equal parts of the following:

Clove
Copal
Dragon's Blood
Garlic
Rue
Sandalwood
Twitch Grass

Reverse Bad Luck Powder No. 2
For purification, money spells and reversing bad luck

1/4 cup Low John (Galangal) root
1/2 tsp. Nasturtium seeds
1/4 cup Patchouli
7 drops Citronella oil
Sprinkling of Holy Water
Copper coin

Combine the above herbs and powder them. Add a few drops of Citronella oil and a sprinkling of Holy Water. Store this mixture in a cool, dark place with a new copper coin in the jar.

Road Opener Powder
For when your efforts seem blocked

Combine and pulverize equal parts of the following:

Abre Camino (Road Opener)
Blue Bonnet
Cedar
Cinnamon
High John the Conqueror
Lemongrass
Nutmeg
Sandalwood

Abre Camino is a critical ingredient in this potion. Its availability may be regional Look for it at botanicas and online stores.

Run Devil Run Powder
To get rid of bad luck

Combine and pulverize equal parts of the following:

Angelica
Black Pepper
Devil's Bit
Dragon's Blood
Flea Bane
Nettles
Red Pepper
Witch Grass

Safe Travel Powder
For safe travel by land or air

Combine and pulverize equal parts of the following:

Calamus Root
Comfrey
Lungwort
Plantain
Salep

Santa Muerte or Holy Death Powder
Protection from sudden death and accidents

Combine and pulverize equal parts of the following:

Devil Pod
Feverfew
Elder flower
Rattle Snake Root

Place this powder in a purple mojo bag or sachet and carry for protection or apply to spells.

Separation Powder No. 1
To break up a couple

1/2 cup Corn Starch
1 T. Black Pepper
1 T. Chili Powder
1 T. Cinnamon
1 T. Low John (Galangal) root
1 T. Vetivert
1 T. Iron Filings

Separation Powder No. 2
To break up a couple

1 tsp. Black Pepper
1 T. Clove
1 T. Sandalwood
1 T. Vetivert

Sleeping Powder

1 T. Catnip
1 T. Hawthorn
2 T. Mugwort
1 T. Skullcap

Stop Harassment Powder

Combine and pulverize equal amounts of the following:

Chili Powder
Cinnamon
Mint
Nutmeg
Tobacco Ashes
Powdered Newsprint

To stop harassment in a certain place, at work for example, sprinkle this powder around the harasser. To stop general and street harassment, place this mixture in a little cloth bag and carry it with you.

Steady Work Powder

Combine and pulverize equal parts of the following:

Bayberry
Benzoin
Gravel Root
Sea Salt

Success in Business Formula No. 1

Combine and pulverize equal parts of the following:

Bayberry
Cedar
Cinnamon
Lilac blossoms
Pine needles
Sandalwood
Spearmint
Violet
Vanilla

Success in Business Formula No. 2

Combine and pulverize equal parts of the following:

Allspice
Basil
Benzoin
Bladderwrack
Dock
Honeysuckle
Juniper berries
Vetivert

Sympathy Powder
To get compassion from others and gain allies

1 tsp. Clovers
1 tsp. Hyacinth
1 tsp. Lavender
1/2 tsp. Lemon peel
2 tsp. Lily petals

Tapa la Boca (Shut Up) No. 1
To stop gossip and slander

Combine and pulverize equal parts of the following:

Adder's Tongue
Chia seeds (available at health food stores)
Clove
Devil's Shoestring
Slippery Elm

Note: This formula is, also, useful when burned as an incense. Speed its action with a little Van Van, Myrrh or Cinnamon.

Tapa la Boca (Shut Up) No. 2

Alum powder
Chia seeds (available at health food stores)
Clove
Slippery Elm

True Love Powder

Combine and pulverize equal parts of the following:

Elecampane
Mistletoe
Verbena

Uncrossing Powder

Combine and pulverize equal parts of the following:

Jasmine
Lemongrass
Violets

Vesta Powder
For banishing

Combine and pulverize equal parts of the following:

Cornmeal
Saltpeter (Warning: Flammable)

Wealthy Way

Combine and pulverize equal parts of the following:

Allspice
Angelica
Cinquefoil (Five Finger Grass)
Frankincense
Jasmine
Nutmeg
Spearmint
Vanilla beans
Add a few drops of White Lotus Oil.

Wishing Powder

Combine and pulverize equal parts of the following:

Cinnamon
Deer's Tongue
Ginseng
Periwinkle
Sage
Sandalwood resin
Sunflower seeds

Cinnamon is optional. It is used here to speed the action of the formula. Deer's Tongue is added to make you more influential in your dealings with others.

9 INCENSE

As given here, these formulas are for very pure, loose incense, which is burned as is or on a charcoal disc such as those sold at metaphysical stores. The advantage of using loose incense without charcoal is that the smoke produced is very pure and untainted by fumes or harsh odors. The disadvantage is that it must be relighted frequently.

The formulas below may be made into cones or other shapes that may remain burning longer by combining herbs, oils and resins with a binder like Gum Tragacanth. There are other binders such as Karaya or Gum Arabic, but Gum Tagacanth is not difficult to find at herb stores or even cake decorating supply shops and it is very versatile. It is mixed with water or other liquids such as an infusion, carrier oil or alcohol to form a sticky substance for your very finely ground herbs and resins. Begin by adding a small amount of liquid to Gum Trgacanth to create a paste of the consistency you would like to work with. You may prefer to use a small hand held blender to get a very smooth consistency.

When combining Gum Tragacanth with your incense formula, use approximately 1/2 to 1 tsp. per 1/2 cup of incense formula. The herbs and resins you use must be ground to a very fine powder for purposes of making this type of incense.

Mix the ingredients thoroughly and mold them in the desired shape. As you work with the mixture, keep a moist cloth on top of the container with the incense mixture, otherwise, it may begin to harden prematurely.

Place the molded shapes on a trap and allow them to dry in a well ventilated place for a day or two depending on how large they are. Naturally, larger ones will take longer to dry than smaller ones. They should be thoroughly dry before you attempt to use them.

Similarly, you may make stick incense by dipping a joss stick or plain incense stick, available from craft shops and incense supply houses, into the mixture. You may have to adjust the consistency to get it to cling properly to the stick.

A very tiny amount of Saltpeter may be added to incense formulas to give them a spark. But, it should be a very small amount in ratio to the total of your incense. For example, begin with a ratio of approximately 1 tsp. Saltpeter to a cup of dried, powdered herb or resin. If you feel you need to add more to get the proper effect, do so sparingly.

Since charcoal discs are usually self-lighting because they are already mixed with Saltpeter, it is not recommended that you use Saltpeter in the recipes if you are using this charcoal. In fact, incense is best when no charcoal is used because there is a reduction in fumes and unpleasant smoke.

It is recommended that if you choose to make use of either charcoal or Saltpeter that you make your first experiments outdoors, on concrete and in a safe environment and that you always use fire safe containers that have lids in case you need to snuff out flames. Keep in mind that both saltpeter and charcoal are ingredients used in the manufacture of gunpowder. Once again, just because they are natural doesn't mean they are entirely safe.

Another option for burning incense more easily on charcoal burners is by adding a few drops of the essential oils called for in a recipe to a small amount of crushed bamboo (bamba) wood base. This is very fine bamboo powder that is available from many herb shops and supply houses. If you have the option of ordering colored base, choose colors that correspond with the purpose of your incense according to the Quick Color Guide at the end of *Chapter 3. Augmenting or Altering the Formulas*.

The easiest, most natural and pure method of using incense is simply as dried, crushed herbs and resins. When you use the formulas in this way, it is not necessary to grind them to an extremely fine powder as you would with other methods. Essential oils may be added to them and they may be tossed onto a small flame in your fireplace or gathered in a safe incense burner and lit with a match or lighter.

General instructions: Grind and mix all of the ingredients together. Store in a cool place inside a glass jar with a tight lid. To use the incense place one or two teaspoons on a charcoal burner and light it.

Special Word of Caution: It cannot be over-emphasized to the novice that charcoal discs become remarkably hot. Always use a metal burner and place it on a marble, brick, ceramic tile or other heat-resistant, non-flammable surface.

These recipes are provided for you to use solely on your own responsibility. When you burn incense, you should always take the precaution of having adequate ventilation and a fire extinguisher nearby. Do not burn incense around people who suffer from respiratory problems.

Aphrodisiac Incense

Combine and pulverize equal parts of the following:

Ambrette or Amber resin
Jasmine
Orange
Rose
Sandalwood

Attract a Dominant Lover Incense

Combine and pulverize equal parts of the following:

Safflower
Sampson Snake root

Better Business Incense
Use this when business is slow

Combine and pulverize equal parts of the following:

Allspice
Anise
Basil
Bay
Cinnamon
Frankincense
Myrrh
Rose
Tonka Bean
Veitvert

Black Cat Incense
For gambling; to reverse bad luck and attract good fortune

Combine and pulverize the following:

1 T. Angelica root
1 T. Cayenne Pepper
2 T. Chamomile
1 T. Rose Geranium
1 T. St. John's Wort
2 T. Solomon's Seal
Pinch of Sea Salt

Consecration Incense

Combine and pulverize equal parts of the following:

Bay leaves
Benzoin
Cypress
Frankincense
Myrrh

Destroy Enemies Incense

1 T. Bone Meal
2 T. Dragon's Blood resin
1/4 tsp. Black Pepper
1 T. Graveyard Dirt (Preferably, gathered at midnight on a waning moon from the grave of a murder.)
1 T. Valerian root

Domination Incense

3 T. Clove
1 T. Calamus root
1 T. Dragon's Blood resin
1 T. Frankincense
2 tsp. Damiana
7 drops Bergamot oil

Fiery Wall of Protection Incense

Combine and pulverize equal parts of the following:

Dragon's Blood
Frankincense
Ginger root
Myrrh
Sea Salt

Home Protection Incense

Combine and pulverize equal parts of the following:

Cinquefoil (Five Finger Grass)
Gardenia blossoms
Purslane
Sandalwood resin

House Blessing Incense

2 T. Lemon peel, dried
1 T. Rosemary
1 T. Cinnamon
1 T. Garlic
1 T. Allspice
1 T. Coconut, dried
1 tsp. Almond extract
Pinch of Sea Salt

License to Depart Incense
To exorcise a spirit after summoning

1 tsp. Frankincense
1 tsp. Thyme

To use this incense properly for an exorcism, allow the Frankincense to burn first, then apply the Thyme to the fire.

Mastering Incense
*To gain control of a situation
and manipulate it to your greatest advantage*

Calamus
Ginger
Ginseng
High John the Conqueror

Necromancy Incense No. 1
To raise the dead

1 tsp. Amber resin
2 T. Benzoin
2 T. Pepperwort
1 tsp. Saffron

Necromancy Incense No. 2
To see the spirits of the dead

2 T. Aloes
2 T. Amber resin
1 T. Black Pepper
1 tsp. Saffron
2 T. Vervain

Ouija Incense
For success with spirit boards

Combine and pulverize equal parts of the following:

Camphor
Cloves

Prosperity Incense

2 T. Bayberry
2 T. Rue
1 T. Cinnamon
1 T. Frankincense
1 T. Nutmeg

Psychic Visions Incense

1 T. Calamus
1 T. Cinnamon
2 T. Gum mastic
2 T. Juniper
1 T. Thyme
Pinch of Amber resin
Pinch of Patchouli

Ritual Incense

Combine and pulverize equal parts of each:

Bergamot
Copal
Cinnamon
Marshmallow root
Bergamot
Frankincense

Run Devil Run Incense
Get rid of bad luck

Combine and pulverize equal parts of the following:

Angelica
Clove
Devil's Bit
Dragon's Blood
Fumitory
Nettles
Thistle
Witch Grass

Saint Expedite Incense
To expedite any operation

Combine and pulverize equal parts of the following:

Allspice powder
Honeysuckle, dried
Sandalwood resin

Saint Martha the Dominator Incense
For controlling, commanding, protection; used by women to command a lover

Calamus root
Dragon's Blood resin
French Tarragon
Hyssop blossoms
Holy Water

Combine equal parts of the above dried, powdered herbs. Sprinkle the mixture with a few drops of Holy Water.

Santeria Incense

2 T. Copal
1 T. Frankincense
1 T. Rosemary

Santa Muerte or Holy Death Returning Incense
To return an errant lover, a missing pet or lost or stolen articles

Cat's Claw
Cinquefoil (Five Finger Grass)
Damiana
Devil's Claw

Scrying Incense
For crystal gazing

2 T. Lavender
2 T. Mugwort
Pinch of Wormwood

Seven African Powers Incense

2 T. Cinnamon powder
1/2 T. Dragon's Blood resin
4 T. Frankincense resin
1 T. Lemon peel, dried
1 T. Orange peel, dried
3 T. Myrrh resin
1 T. Sandalwood resin
1 T. White Sage powder

Space Clearing Incense

Combine and pulverize equal parts of the following:

Cedar
Rosemary
Sage
Thyme
Sea Salt

Spiritual Assistance Incense
To call benevolent spirits

Combine and pulverize equal parts of the following:

Cinnamon
Clove
Ginger
Rosemary
Thyme

Summoning Incense
To summon angels, including the fallen ones

Combine and pulverize equal parts of the following:

Balm of Gilead
Calamus
Copal
Myrrh

Temple Incense

3 T. Frankincense
2 T. Lavender
2 T. Myrrh
1 T. Sandalwood

Transformation Incense
For making changes and transitions

Combine and pulverize equal parts of the following:

Birthwort
Cinquefoil (Five Finger Grass)
Sage
Stonecrop

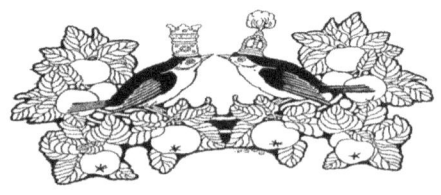

True Love Incense
To attract a pure and long-lasting love

1 tsp. Cinnamon
2 T. Copal resin
2 T. Damiana

White Light of Protection Incense

Combine and pulverize equal parts of the following:

Bay leaves
Eucalyptus
Fern
Ginger root
Holly
Sea Salt

Winter Solstice Incense

Combine and pulverize equal parts of the following:

Grapefruit peel, dried
Lemon peel, dried
Orange peel, dried
Tangerine peel, dried

10 WASHES AND BATHS

Make your washes and baths as you would a tea or decoction. When the water cools, strain the herbs and other ingredients out and bottle it.

Use washes to mop or scrub your floors, walls, porch, sidewalk and other hard surfaces at your home or business with it or to use it as a bath for yourself by pouring one to two cups into your bath water. You may use washes alone or add them to your usual floor cleaning liquid.

Bath formulas can be turned into bathing salts by mixing and crushing the dried ingredients or essential oils in the formula together with sea salt or Epsom salts. You may, also, add the essential oils to plain Castille or other unscented liquid body soap.

If you have surfaces that cannot be mopped or scrubbed, but you'd like to use a wash, you may do so by placing the formula in a spray bottle. It is important that you strain the mixture through a coffee filter or other fine filter so that it doesn't clog the sprayer.

Washes will keep for 3 to 4 days in your refrigerator. If you'd like to keep them longer, add a small amount of Vodka or other grain alcohol to the bottle as a preservative.

For best results use purifying, banishing and exorcism

formulas before using those to attract luck, love or prosperity.

Banish Evil Spirits Wash or Bath

1 gallon pure Water
1 cup Sage
1/2 cup Pine Needles
1/4 cup Cloves
1/4 cup Violet blossoms
2 T. Cinnamon
1 T. Sea Salt

Black Cat Wash or Bath
For gambling; to dispel bad luck and draw good luck

Angelica root
Cayenne Pepper
Chamomile
Rose Geranium
St. John's Wort
Solomon's Seal
Pinch of Sea Salt

Optionally, add Cinnamon and Bergamot to reverse bad luck and bring customers to your business.

Chinese Wash
To draw good customers to your business

1 quart Water
13 Broomcorn straws
6 oz. liquid Castille soap
3 oz. Van Van Oil

Boil the Broomcorn straws in water. Allow it to cool. Remove the Broomcorn straws. Add the remaining ingredients.

Exorcism Wash or Bath
For purification

1 gallon pure Water
1/2 cup of Rosemary
1/4 cup Bay leaves
1/4 cup White Clover blossoms
1/4 cup Eucalyptus

Fast Luck Wash
To bring customers into a business

1 quart pure Water
1 tsp. Bergamot oil
1 tsp. Cinnamon oil
1 tsp. Citronella oil

Combine in a jar and shake thoroughly.

Fast Scrubbing Essence Wash
To attract customers to a business

Anise
Bergamot
Cinnamon
Dragon's Blood
Frankincense
Geranium
Hyssop
Lavender
Lemongrass
Myrrh
Orange Flowers
Rosemary
Wintergreen

This formula is based on a 13-herb Fast Scrubbing Essence formula given by Zora Neale Hurston in Men and Mules.[23] Add it to your usual washing solution or use it alone to wipe down the floors, walls and sidewalks of your business to attract customers.

There are two ways to create this wash. You may use 3 to 5 drops of each of the essential oils in a quart of pure water. Or, boil approximately 1/4 cup of each of the dried or fresh herbs in approximately a gallon of water. Make a strong decoction by allowing the brew to simmer for 10 minutes. Allow it to cool. Strain it and apply it with a mop or wash cloth.

House Protection Wash

1 gallon pure Water
1/2 cup Peppermint
1/4 cup Angelica root
1/4 cup Basil
1/4 cup Hyssop
1/4 cup Sage

Love and Harmony Wash or Bath

1 Gallon pure Water
1/2 cup Red Rose petals
1/4 cup African Violets
1/4 cup Clover
1/4 cup Crocus
1/4 cup Elecampane
1/4 cup Lemon Verbena
1 T. Cinnamon

Money Drawing No. 1 Wash or Bath

1 gallon of pure Water
1/4 cup Basil
1/4 cup Bayberry
1/4 cup Cinnamon
1/4 cup Cloves
1/4 cup Nutmeg
1/4 cup Rue

Money Drawing No. 2 Wash or Bath

1 gallon of pure Water
1/2 cup Basil
1/2 cup Coltsfoot
1/2 cup Rue

Protection from Thieves Wash or Bath

1 quart of pure Water
3 T. Frankincense resin
1/4 cup Juniper berries
1/4 Vetivert
1 T. Cumin

Seven African Powers Wash or Bath

1 gallon pure Water
1/4 cup Abre Camino herb (available at Cuban botanicas and online)
1/4 cup Gardenia Flowers
1/4 cup Peppermint
1/4 cup Rosemary
1/4 cup Violets
3 T. Allspice

Abre Camino (Open the Road) is an important herb in this formula.

Tranquility Wash or Bath

1 gallon pure Water
1/4 cup Chamomile
1/4 cup Lavender
1/4 cup Lemongrass
1/4 cup Skullcap
1/4 cup Thyme

Uncrossing Wash or Bath

Combine equal parts of the following:

1 gallon pure Water
Chamomile
Hyacinth
Hyssop
Lavender
Rue
Sage
Solomon's Seal
Twitch Grass
Vetivert
Woodruff

Hyssop, Rue, Lavender and Sage are among the most important herbs in this formula. For uncrossing, this bath is used 7-days straight. It is customary to light two white candles anointed with Uncrossing Oil and recite the 51st Psalm. This formulary, also, makes a good purification bath before conducting rituals and spells. Use as a wash to purify your home or business of adversarial vibrations.

REFERENCES

1. Alibeck the Egyptian, "Grimoirum Verum," 1517.

2. Crowley, Aleister, "The Book of the Law (Technically called Liber AL vel Legis sub figura CCXX as delivered by XCIII = 418 to DCLXVI)", Samuel Weiser, York Beach, ME, 1977.

3. Mathers, S.L. MacGregor, Translator, "The Book of the Sacred Magic of Abramelin the Mage," Dover Publications, 1975.

4. Granger, Mary, District Supervisor, Georgia Writer's Project, "Drums and Shadows," 1940.
http://www.sacred-texts.com/afr/das/index.htm

5. Hurston, Zora Neale, "Mules and Men," 1935.

6. Godey, Louis Antoine and Sarah Josepha Buell Hale, Ed., "Godey's Lady's Book, Volume 56, 1858.

7. Ibid.

8. Hurston, Zora Neale, "Mules and Men," 1935.

9. Ibid.

10. Ruiz, Ruel N., "Potions, Gayuma, Atbp.Kuwento ng Pag aaral ni Satohri", P. 73. Retrieved on 5/20/2012. http://www.scribd.com/ruel_ruiz_1/d/83260076-Potions-Gayuma-Atbp

11. Ruiz, Ruel N., "Elemental, Enkanto, Atbp.Of Man and Myths: Philippine Lower Mythology Ghouls and Creatures of Darkness, Elementals and Demons," Pp. 31-34. http://www.scribd.com/ruel_ruiz_1/d/83234069/80-mangabarang

12. Begy, Joseph A., "Practical Handbook of Toilet Preparations and Their Uses, Also Recipes for the Household," New York: Wm. L. Allison, Publishing, 1889. Pp. 138-139.

13. Kelley, Thomas, "Household Cyclopedia of General Information, Containing Over 10,000 Receipts, In All the Useful and Domestic Arts, Constituting a Complete and Practical Library, Relating to Agriculture, Angling, Bees, Bleaching, Keeping, Brewing" New York, 1881.

14. Salverte, Eusebe, "The Occult Sciences: The Philosophy of Magic, Prodigies, and Apparent Miracles," New York: Harper and Brothers Publishers, 1847, P. 41.

15. Hurston, Zora Neale, "Mules and Men," 1935.

16 Granger, Mary, District Supervisor, Georgia Writer's Project, "Drums and Shadows," 1940, P. 15-16.
http://www.sacred-texts.com/afr/das/index.htm

17. Bardon, Franz, Trans. A. Radspieler, "Initiation Into Hermetics: A Course of Instruction of Magic Theory & Practice," Dieter Ruggeberg, 1971.

18. Mooney, James, "Myths of the Cherokee", Dover Publishing, 1995, Pp. 271–273, 232–236, 450. Reprinted from a Government Printing Office publication of 1900.

19. Hurston, Zora Neale, "Mules and Men," 1935.

20. Ibid.

21. Begy, Joseph A., "Practical Handbook of Toilet Preparations and Their Uses, Also Recipes for the Household," New York: Wm. L. Allison, Publishing, 1889. Pp. 166-167.

22. Ibid.

23. Hurston, Zora Neale, "Mules and Men," 1935.

Sophia diGregorio

ABBREVIATIONS AND CONVERSIONS OF MEASUREMENTS

Abbreviation Key for Measurements

T. = Tablespoon
tsp. = teaspoon
oz. = ounce
g = gram
ml = milliliter

Conversion of Measurements

3 tsp. = 1 T.
1 cup = 16 T.
1 cup = 8 oz.
1 pint =16 oz.
1 pint = 2 cups
1 tsp. = approximately 4.2 g
1 cup liquid = approximately 220 to 240 g
1 cup non-liquid = approximately 120 to 140 g
1 dram = 1/8 oz. = 60 grams = 3.697 ml = 60 drops
1 dram = .125 fl. oz. or approximately 3/4 tsp.
1 pint = approximately 473 ml
1 ml = 15 drops of liquid

Sophia diGregorio

OTHER WINTER TEMPEST BOOKS

If you enjoyed this book, you might enjoy other Winter Tempest Books:

All Natural Dental Remedies: Herbs and Home Remedies to Heal Your Teeth & Naturally Restore Tooth Enamel by Angela Kaelin

Black Magic for Dark Times: Spells of Revenge and Protection by Angela Kaelin

Blood and Black Roses: A Dark Bouquet of Vampires, Romance and Horror by Sophia diGregorio (Fiction)

The Forgotten: The Vampire Prince by Sophia diGregorio

How to Communicate with Spirits: Séances, Ouija Boards and Summoning by Angela Kaelin

How to Develop Advanced Psychic Abilities: Obtain Information about the Past, Present and Future Through Clairvoyance by Sophia diGregorio

How to Read the Tarot for Fun, Profit and Psychic Development for Beginners and Advanced Readers by Angela Kaelin

How to Write Your Own Spells for Any Purpose and Make Them Work by Sophia diGregorio

Magical Healing: How to Use Your Mind to Heal Yourself and Others by Angela Kaelin

Natural Remedies for Reversing Gray Hair: Nutrition and Herbs for Anti-aging and Optimum Health by Thomas W. Xander

Practical Black Magic: How to Hex and Curse Your Enemies by Sophia diGregorio

Spells for Money and Wealth by Angela Kaelin

To Conjure the Perfect Man by Sophia diGregorio (Fiction)

The Traditional Witches' Book of Love Spells by Angela Kaelin

Disclaimer: The author and publisher of this guide has used her best efforts in preparing this document. The author makes no representation or warranties with respect to the accuracy, applicability, fitness or completeness of the contents of this document. The author disclaims any warranties expressed or implied. The author of this book is not a medical or legal professional and is not qualified to give medical or legal advice. Nothing in this document should be construed as medical or legal advice. The material in this book is presented for informational purposes only. Nothing in this book should be construed as incitement to dangerous or illegal acts and the reader is advised to be aware of and heed all pertinent laws in his or her city, state, country or other jurisdiction. Any medical or legal questions should be addressed to the proper medical or legal authorities. The author shall in no event be held liable for any losses or damages, including but not limited to special, incidental, consequential or other damages incurred by the use of this information. The statements in this book have not been evaluated by any government organization. The statements contained herein represent the legally protected opinions of the author and are presented for informational purposes only. Anyone who uses any of the information in the book does so at their own risk with the understanding that the author cannot be held responsible for the consequences. This document contains material protected under copyright laws. Any unauthorized reprint, transmission or resale of this material without the express permission of the author is strictly prohibited.

FTC Disclaimer: The author has no connection to nor was paid by any brand or product described in this document with the exception of any other books mentioned which were written by the author or published by Winter Tempest Books.

www.ingramcontent.com/pod-product-compliance
Lightning Source LLC
Chambersburg PA
CBHW032041090426
42744CB00004B/86